UNHEALTHY:

CORRUPTION, MALPRACTICE, AND COVID-19 IN THE AMERICAN HEALTH SYSTEM

UNHEALTHY:

CORRUPTION, MALPRACTICE, AND COVID-19 IN THE AMERICAN HEALTH SYSTEM

RICHARD L. KRADIN, M.D., DTM&H
HARVARD MEDICAL SCHOOL, PROFESSOR EMERITUS

DEFIANCE PRESS
& PUBLISHING

Unhealthy: Corruption, Malpractice, and Covid-19 In the American Health System

ISBN-13: 978-1-955937-22-1 (Paperback)
ISBN-13: 978-1-955937-21-4 (eBook)

Published by Defiance Press and Publishing, LLC

Bulk orders of this book may be obtained by contacting Defiance Press and Publishing, LLC. www.defiancepress.com.

Public Relations Dept. – Defiance Press & Publishing, LLC
281-581-9300
pr@defiancepress.com

Defiance Press & Publishing, LLC
281-581-9300
info@defiancepress.com

ACKNOWLEDGEMENTS

I would like to thank my colleagues who have come under attack for insisting on telling the truth despite it not being safe to do so throughout this extended pandemic.

Thank you to family and friends who encouraged me to write this text.

And thank you to Rafi, the cutest dog on the planet, who told me when it was time to stop writing and start playing.

TABLE OF CONTENTS

PART I: CORRUPTION

I do plainly and ingenuously confess that I am guilty of corruption, and do renounce all defense.

—Francis Bacon

I have said to corruption, thou art my father. To the worm, thou art my mother and my sister.

—Job 17:14

INTRODUCTION

In the winter of 2019/2020, the world witnessed the global spread of a new and deadly viral infection. Unfortunately, the public health response to the COVID-19 pandemic was muddled, resulting in needless pain and suffering for Americans of all ages. What follows is the story of the pandemic and how it was mishandled. It examines the thirty-year transformation of American medicine from a profession to a "woke" corporate system, one that appears more concerned with profit, politics, and political correctness than with public health. I have chosen to tell the story because I practiced academic medicine for over forty years as a Harvard physician and witnessed what went wrong.

In his 1960 farewell address to the nation, President Dwight Eisenhower warned that a "military-industrial complex" was threatening to corrupt society. Today, as the viral pandemic rages on, America is witnessing its health system being undermined by corporate and political influences. An ideologically-driven disregard for truth has led many American physicians to ignore the scientific precepts they were trained to safeguard. Tasked with guiding the public through a pandemic, they have repeatedly blundered, by offering confusing messages and false information concerning its risks and how to combat it.

Americans have been led to believe that the current pandemic could not have been predicted and consequently, the medical profession was not prepared to confront it. But whereas SARS-CoV2 (COVID-19) is a novel virus, physicians have accumulated substantial experience with how viral respiratory pandemics tend to behave. When empirical data began to emerge concerning who was vulnerable to the lethal effects of the virus and who was not, any element of surprise should have quickly dissipated, and health policies appropriately adjusted based on data. But this did not occur.

Soon after COVID-19 was first detected in the winter of 2019/20, it became obvious that the aged and sick were at risk of developing severe disease but that everyone else, especially the healthy young, was at low risk of dying from the virus or of spreading it. Despite this, health experts insisted on approaching the entire population as though they were sick octogenarians. A pandemic that could have been competently and fairly simply managed was instead allowed to shut down the American economy. People's rights were trampled, and the education of America's youth was ignored. The government-mandated drive to vaccinate the entire population ignored age, immune status, and the possible deleterious side-effects of novel vaccines. Masking policies and wide-scale lockdowns were instituted with no significant beneficial effect.

Today, an increasingly skeptical public has begun to appreciate that they were misinformed and frankly lied to. Governmental health policies did not "follow the science." Instead, Americans have witnessed a policy driven by incompetence, greed, and callous indifference. As a result, the reputation of the medical profession and science, in general, has been seriously damaged.

Having trained extensively in the field of medicine, I watched with burgeoning frustration how the pandemic was being mishandled. I *knew* that the messaging from our government's health experts was not based on science. Instead, it was a reflection of a series of corrosive changes that have occurred in the field of medicine over the last thirty years. Many of these changes have been driven by greed, and largely out of public view, but the stress of the pandemic has exposed them, and today they can be recognized by anyone with "eyes to see."

AN AUTOBIOGRAPHICAL PERSPECTIVE

I am a member of America's medical "elite." I say that not to boast but because it is true. I am a Harvard-trained academic physician and medical school professor. I lived in Concord, Massachusetts, "ground zero" for Progressive ideology in New England. The town of Concord is an example of everything that is right and wrong with Progressive America. An idyllic elite suburb with a rich history, it was home to Emerson, Thoreau, and the Alcotts. It is populated largely by professors from Harvard and MIT, as well as by corporate CEOs. Progressive to the core, the "Black Lives Matter (BLM)" logo is ubiquitously displayed on the town's lawn signs, and on the banners that drape the façades of its churches. Yet few blacks live in Concord, MA., and its townspeople rarely have direct dealings with "peoples of color," other than their gardeners, nannies, and house cleaners.

I share much in common on paper with my neighbors, but my background likely differs from theirs. I was raised in a blue-collar neighborhood in New York City. Neither of my parents attended college, but they taught me that success was achieved through hard work and "common sense." When I entered the New York City public school system, students were required to take aptitude tests in math and science. It was the early 1960s, and America was in a post-Sputnik race with the Soviet Union to educate future scientists. I scored well on the tests and was assigned to a "special" high school class for gifted students.

I had a diverse group of friends. Some were "smart," others not terribly so. But I found something to relate to in all of them. However, my fellow students in the "special science" classes were not as welcoming to those outside their circle. They were proud of their superior status— snobs, whose favorite pastime was denigrating "ordinary" students, who they spoke of with disdain. At the time, I didn't appreciate that they would become America's elite.

I attended medical school, completed my medical training in Boston, and assumed my life's professional role as a Harvard physician and professor. I arrived at Harvard with the expectation of meeting exceptionally talented people, and although I did meet some, the percentage was small. What most shared in common was a penchant for hard work and pride in being part of a prestigious institution.

Civilizations have always had their elites. But what distinguished America from its various cousins was that its people disapproved of pretensions of superiority based on class. But in the twenty-first century, elites have begun to claim openly what they view as their rightful role as America's leaders. This includes the medical elite charged with guiding the nation's health policy.

THE GREAT MEDICAL RESET

In the 1990s, the field of medicine was transformed into corporate business. I recall the new CEO of *Partners Health*— the corporate health system created by the merger of the two largest Harvard-affiliated hospitals— addressing the medical staff and announcing that to cut costs and improve efficiency, the "leadership"—a term previously never used— was planning on introducing standardized algorithms for the treatment of various diseases. The goal was to reduce hospital costs. As a result, individual physician choices as to treatment would be discouraged in favor of the standardized ones. To accomplish this, physicians would have to help formulate the guidelines, while the hospital leadership would continue in its role as "visionaries" for the hospital's future. At the time, I naively assumed that my colleagues would resist this intrusion on their autonomy. But I was wrong. Instead, they eagerly volunteered to help and were quick to divest their traditional freedoms to serve at the new "leadership's" bidding.

Over the next thirty years, the hospital and the medical profession-at-large moved along a path of rigid hierarchy and authoritarianism. The social and economic distance between the "leadership" and the working staff increased, and a slew of new regulations was imposed. When computers came online, they were used to monitor the behaviors and efficiency of the staff, something that had never been possible before. Increasingly, the corporate medical system aligned itself with Progressive ideology, endorsing its pseudoscientific notions about race, gender, diversity, and equity. Today, there are physicians who see "social justice," as a medical *raison d'etre*. The once dispassionate physician morphed into a "woke" activist, as concerned with "micro-aggressions" as with the health of patients.

CHAPTER ONE: THE CULTURAL MILIEU

I am a Liberal, yet I am Liberal tempered by experience, reflection, and renouncement, and I am above all, a believer in culture.

—Matthew Arnold

Cultural memory binds the present to the past. In its absence, it is impossible to reference the present or predict the future. Without the stabilizing influence of history, any society can be expected to lose its moorings. But history is no longer taught or practiced in a coherent manner. As historian Niall Ferguson notes in *Civilization*:

> For roughly thirty years, young people at Western schools and universities have been given the *idea* of a liberal education, without the *substance* of historical knowledge. They have been taught isolated "modules," not narratives, much less chronologies....They have been encouraged to feel empathy with imagined Roman centurions and Holocaust victims, not to write essays about why and how their predicaments arose. (Ferguson, 2011) *xix* (present author's italics)

My father was born in the first decade of the twentieth century. When I was a boy, he would tell me about the world of his youth. He spoke of fire engines drawn by horses, a place without automobiles, radio, television, or airplanes. He recalled family members who had died from the "Spanish flu," tuberculosis, and diabetes, in a time before effective antibiotics and insulin.[1] His life had been harder than mine, as in my America, disease, war, and famine were not pressing realities.

Instead, the America of my youth in the 1950s was a placid place. We had recently won the War and saved the world from fascism; we were proud and patriotic. But this time appeared to end suddenly in 1963 when John Kennedy was assassinated. By the time I entered university in 1967, the Vietnam War was in full gear and there was widespread mistrust of Government amongst America's students. I participated, in retrospect rather mindlessly, in the student protests in Washington, DC, and on Wall Street.

I witnessed the violence of the "hard-hat riots" in 1970 on Wall Street, led by disgruntled blue-collar workers, angered by the unpatriotic stances of America's rebellious youth.[2] At the time, I never questioned whether the demonstrations against the war might have been ill conceived. It did not dawn on me that Progressive education and culture had unconsciously left me with a Leftist worldview, or that my actions were being shaped by unseen political forces.

Following the Civil Rights movement of the '60s, it appeared that America was becoming a more tolerant nation.[3] Fifty years later, America elected its first black president, and most assumed that racial discrimination was a thing of the past. Instead, Barack Obama's

---

1   The Model T automobile was introduced by Henry Ford in 1918. Air travel began in the 1920s. The first radio broadcast was in 1920. The first television broadcast was in 1927. The Spanish Influenza epidemic began in 1917. Insulin was introduced in 1921. Effective chemotherapy for tuberculosis was not available until the 1950s.

2   The so-called "hard hat riots" that occurred in lower Manhattan were a culmination of the frustration that patriotic blue-collar workers felt about the blatant disrespect toward authority that long-haired pot smoking college students were openly expressing during these years. The New York City Police did little to protect the demonstrators from the violent attack of hard-hatted tradesmen. These events have been elucidated in a recent book by David Kuhn, The Hardhat Riot: Nixon, New York City, and the Dawn of the White Working-Class Revolution.2020. Oxford

3   Any honest person who lived before the 1960s will attest to the fact that America has made great strides toward addressing the issue of racism. The notion that the country is "systemically racist" certainly does not jibe with my own experience.

Presidency plunged America into increased cultural and racial polarization.[4] Other changes were also occurring in America. Corporations were growing larger, and an increasingly powerful managerial class, devoted to its own financial success, was creating large wealth disparities amongst Americans. The middle class, ostensibly critical to the success of a democratic republic, was shrinking, and less than 1 percent of Americans now held more than 90 percent of the nation's wealth. The Reagan years of the 1980s ushered in a period of unbridled materialism and greed, as depicted in Hollywood by Oliver Stone's *Wall Street*, Martin Scorsese's *Wolf of Wall Street*, and David Mamet's *Glengarry Glen Ross*. The increased national debt and limited job opportunities virtually guaranteed that for the first time in American history, children would not outperform their parents at any level.

America's youth was growing disenchanted with the failed promises of capitalism. With the help of Progressive education, they were beginning to consider socialism as a potential path toward improving their future. However, few were properly informed about the dismal history of socialism when tried in practice. Post-modern scholars in the academy routinely applied Marxist critical theory to divide society into "oppressor" and "oppressed" classes, on a host of cultural issues (Di'Souza, 2020). What had been near-moribund racism in America was resuscitated by Marxists in the pursuit of undermining the capitalist system. The promise of social "equity" was offered as an alternative to traditional notions of legal "equality" and merit-based achievement. The digital technological revolution allowed the Internet and social media giants, including *Facebook*, *Twitter*, and *Google*, to provide a platform for the disgruntled, who expressed strong opinions, albeit often with little expertise, on virtually any topic. A troubling coop-

---

4   Few questioned that Obama was bi-racial or that his father was African. His family has not been slaves in a racist America. His having black skin was enough to ease the collective guilt of Americans.

eration emerged between technology companies and the Progressive Democratic Party that threatened free speech and raised the specter of one-party totalitarian rule.

Progressivism, a political ideology, originally wedded to a rational scientific approach to governance, was infiltrated by hostile polemics against the rule of law. Calls for political correctness, an end to "white privilege," and defunding police strained the fabric of American society. At the same time, science was making other technological strides. Following the discovery of DNA in the 1950s, the ability to manipulate the genome raised serious ethical concerns and pitted secular humanism against traditional religion. Heady intellectuals, like Yuval Noah Hariri, questioned whether the human race would continue to exist or be replaced by hybrid forms of computer-enhanced bionic life in the near future.[5] (Hariri, 2020)

MEDICAL MALPRACTICE

Physicians have a stake in Progressivism's vision of a better world through science. Historically, medicine was both a prime mover and beneficiary of the eighteenth-century Enlightenment. The primary goal of the Enlightenment was to replace irrational ideas and practices with a scientific worldview. This included an empirical, rather than *a priori* dogmatic, appreciation of the human body, manifesting efforts to heal the sick in reliable and reproducible ways. But the *philosophes* of the Enlightenment failed to recognize that "irrationality" is not something that can be expunged. Instead, it is an integral part of man's psychological repertoire, the legacy of a bicameral mind that pits the logic of the "left brain" against the imagination of the right. The irrational is *real,* and it comes to the fore spontaneously, when cognitive activi-

---

5   Hariri's vision for the future, one apparently shared by Bill Gates and other technocrats, is frankly frightening. It suggests how bizarre the direction of humanity may become in the absence of meaningful moral structures.

ties are diminished during times of anxiety and emotional distress. Nevertheless, physicians are expected to exclude the irrational from their approach to medical practice.

Despite their stated adherence to rational science, many ideas fostered by Progressives are patently irrational. There is perhaps no better example of this than the current notion of "gender fluidity." Today, America's major medical societies uniformly support the notion that ill-defined "gender" determines human sexuality. This is in keeping with post-deconstructionist arguments within the academy that there is no such thing as objective truth, and that reality can be "framed" subjectively based on one's longings. Progressives contend that gender is "fluid" and potentially can change at any time based on one's feelings and that with the assistance of medical science, gender and secondary sexual characteristics can be realigned. It is comparable to what psychologists call a "state" rather than a "trait," meaning that it is not fixed but prone to change. The problem is that there is not a shred of empirical scientific evidence to support this notion, and until recently, it would have been dismissed as absurd, at best.

Yet, today there are physicians, trained in medical science, who are allowing young children to make life-altering surgical decisions in response to normal adolescent sexual confusion and neurotic parental pressures.[6] Consider the following statement from the Boston Children's Hospital website:

> Gender dysphoria occurs when there is a conflict between the gender
> you were assigned at birth and the gender with which you identify.

---

6 The phenomenon of parents, usually mothers, insisting that their young children undergo gender reassignment would in the past have been classified as "Munchausen disorder by proxy" in which a parent forces a child to undergo unnecessary and potentially harmful medical and surgical procedures due to an unconscious wish to harm the child, lash out at the "opposite sex" or keep the child dependent. It is a form of child abuse and should be taken seriously. In such cases, the child should be separated from the offending parent. But today, such parents are protected by a perverse ideology wedded to the idea that gender is a choice that a parent can make for a young child and by Progressive judges, who have ruled in favor of such mothers.

This can create significant distress, and you may feel uncomfortable in your body. The Center for Gender Surgery at Boston Children's Hospital offers gender affirmation surgery services to eligible adolescents and young adults who are ready to take this step in their journey. It is the first center of its kind in the US in a major pediatric hospital setting. adolescents and young adults who are ready to take this step in their journey. It is the first center of its kind in the US in a major pediatric hospital setting. ("Center for Gender Surgery Boston Children's Hospital," 2021)

For physicians to accept emotionally driven subjective evaluations above objective signs of sexual differentiation reflects a willingness to embrace ideology over empirical facts. Physicians who profess such ideas are effectively divesting themselves of their professional responsibilities, and abandoning their role as scientists in favor of cultural activism. They are disobeying the ethical core of the Hippocratic Oath, which is to do no harm, by denying the known physical and psychological complications of gender-reassignment procedures. Simply put, in their newfound role as cultural zealots, they are committing malpractice.

Consider a report concerning the results of gender-reassignment surgery from a French medical center in 2019:

In primary male to female (MTF) sex reassignment surgery (SRS), the most frequent postoperative functional complications using the penoscrotal skin technique remain neovaginal stenosis, urinary meatal stenosis, and secondary revision surgery.... Among the 189 included patients, we reported a 2.6 percent of rectovaginal wall perforations. In 37 percent of patients, we had repeated compressive dressings and 15 percent of them required blood transfusions. Eighteen percent of patients presented with hematoma and 27 percent with early infectious complications. Delayed short-depth neovagina occurred in 21 percent of patients, requiring additional hard dilatation, with a 95.5 percent success rate. Total secondary vaginoplasty rate was 6.3 percent (4.7 percent skin graft and 3.7 percent bowel plasty). Secondary functional meatoplasty occurred in

1 percent of cases. Other secondary cosmetic surgery rates ranged between 3 to 20 percent.... Secondary vaginoplasty was required in cases of neovagina stenosis ...(Cristofari, Bertrand, Leuzzi, & al, 2019)

Obviously, these "elective procedures" that are being advertised as benign can have severe life-threatening complications.

Despite this, the American Medical Association (AMA) and the American Psychological Associations (APA) have steadfastly supported gender reassignment. They have suppressed information concerning the dangers of these surgeries, and instead have chosen to limit their attention to cases with salutary outcomes. Recently, a transgendered physician acknowledged the psychological and relational difficulties that can persist after re-assignment surgery:

Surgery and hormonal therapy are increasingly common treatments for gender dysphoria, but the prejudice and discrimination transgender individuals face post-transition can cause significant psychological distress, says Marci Bowers, MD, a surgeon who performs gender reassignment surgery in Trinidad, Colo., and is herself transgender.

Post-change, many men and women deal with rancorous divorces, custody battles, job loss, and rejection by family members, she has found. Some even commit suicide, continues Bowers, who will speak about the psychological impact of transgender surgery at APA's 2007 Annual Convention. "It's a wonder that anyone transitions—the penalties are so severe," she says. (Meyers, 2020)

I know this to be true because I have personally treated transgender patients in psychotherapy, and can attest that *all* had concomitant serious mental issues that were not resolved by gender-altering surgeries. These included pathological narcissism, borderline levels of abandonment anxiety, drug addiction, and self-destructive behaviors, none of which improved following gender reassignment surgery.

Dr. Paul McHugh, the long-time Chief of Psychiatry at the Johns

Hopkins Medical Center, argued for years about the dangers of normalizing gender confusion, likening the current trend to allowing the "inmates to run the asylum." But in recent years, McHugh has been disparaged by his Progressive medical colleagues. A recent article notes that Johns Hopkins Hospital has now "moved past," McHugh's "antiquated" and "bigoted" opinions:

> Nearly four decades after he derailed a pioneering transgender program at Johns Hopkins Hospital with his views on "guilt-ridden homosexual men," psychiatrist Paul McHugh is seeing his institution come full circle with the resumption of gender-reassignment surgeries. McHugh, the hospital's chief of psychiatry from 1975 to 2001, still believes that being transgender is largely a psychological problem, not a biological phenomenon. And with the title of university distinguished service professor at Johns Hopkins Medicine, he continues to wield enormous influence in certain circles and is quoted frequently on gender issues in conservative media. "I'm not against transgender people," he said recently, stressing that he is "anxious they get the help they need." But such help should be psychiatric rather than surgical, he maintains.
>
> Hopkins, however, is moving beyond McHugh. This summer, it will formally open a transgender health service and will resume, after a thirty-eight-year hiatus, an accompanying surgical program. Once at the forefront of gender-identity science—and site of the nation's first "change-of-sex operations," as the headlines announced in 1966—Hopkins abruptly halted those surgeries in 1979. (Nutt, 2017)

In "moving beyond" objective truth, physicians at Hopkins and elsewhere have sacrificed scientific objectivity on the altar of the culture wars, arguably not a place where medicine is meant to be practiced.

The effects of physicians peddling Progressive ideological stances on the pediatric population are potentially disastrous. Any responsible parent knows that children are impressionable and ill-equipped to make complex life-altering medical decisions. This is why we do not allow children to vote, drink, purchase guns, etc., until they are at least eighteen. A normal child can be expected to change his or her mind frequently on any number of issues. It is a normal and almost always temporary phase for a boy to want to play with dolls, or for a girl to dress like a boy. But the AMA has ignored these commonsensical facts, in favor of the following position:

> In a letter to the National Governors Association (NGA), the AMA cited evidence that trans- and non-binary gender identities are normal variations of human identity and expression, and that forgoing gender-affirming care can have tragic health consequences, both mental and physical.
>
> Decisions about medical care belong within the sanctity of the patient-physician relationship," the AMA wrote in its letter. "As with all medical interventions, physicians are guided by their ethical duty to act in the best interest of their patients and must tailor recommendations about specific interventions and the timing of those interventions to each patient's unique circumstances. Such decisions must be sensitive to the child's clinical situation, nurture the child's short and long-term development, and balance the need to preserve the child's opportunity to make important life choices autonomously in the future. We believe it is inappropriate and harmful for any state to legislatively dictate that certain transition-related services are never appropriate and limit the range of options physicians and families may consider when making decisions for pediatric patients. (AMA, 2021)

There is *no* credible scientific evidence that "trans and non-binary" gender identities are normal psychosocial variations. Despite what some Leftist academics have argued, the notion of normality is not bigoted, rather, society is expected to establish norms if it is to function. "Normal" is a statistical concept that indicates the *mean* or *average* within a group. Whereas the percentage of Americans (0.6 percent) claiming transgender status has increased dramatically in recent years—data would suggest almost certainly due to an increased accommodation to peer pressure—it is by no means sufficiently prevalent to be considered a "norm." Even if one chooses to dispose of statistical measures of "normality" in favor of subjective terms like "health," "well-being," or "diversity," there is still no indication that transgenderism qualifies as any of these categories; rather, there is substantial evidence to suggest that it does not. The argument that one must support gender reassignment for fear that a small fraction of society may be stigmatized makes little sense and denies human nature. There may be cases in which such an intervention is judged to be appropriate, but that is a far cry from making efforts to popularize or normalize this approach.

Arguments that transgenderism is biologically determined do not square with the evidence. Despite occasional studies that have suggested that changes in the hypothalamus can determine gender that might not concord with biological sex, the evidence is by no means compelling (Aeyung, Baron-Cohen, E., & al, 2009). Nor does it exclude an important role for environmental influences. Statistics show that the percentage of Americans claiming transgenderism and homosexuality is inversely related to age. For example, "baby boomers" are far less likely to profess transgender status than millennials or those in Gen Z. This suggests that variant sexuality is primarily culturally rather than biologically determined (Statista, 2021). As one psychologist summarized the issue:

> To be sure, parents often do treat biological boys and girls differently in anticipation of fairly predictable sex and gender differences that are biologically determined. However, such socialization behaviors appear to have little actual causal impact on gender identity.... Unfortunately, in pursuit of the admirable goal of greater sensitivity and inclusivity for individuals whose gendered behaviors do not meet societal expectations, some advocates created a myth that gender identity is divorced from biological factors and can be shaped powerfully by socialization alone. (C. Ferguson, 2021)

Progressive ideologues argue that nature cannot be allowed to limit the spectrum of human experience, and tend to refer positively to biology only when it supports their preferred narratives. The truth is that transgenderism is an imaginal condition, and gender re-assignment is a crude and frankly grotesque effort at altering nature. Any physician who chooses to base his practice on Progressive ideology rather than biologically-determined objective reality forfeits scientific credibility on the altar of "political correctness." Policy proclamations like the one by the AMA are not statements of science; rather they are propaganda that endangers the physical and mental health of vulnerable young people who should be protected from ideological predation. Other positions currently endorsed by mainstream medical societies that decry "white fragility" or "toxic masculinity," or insist that hospitals *must* have unisex bathrooms, represent nothing other than wholesale surrender by the medical profession to politically correct cultural pressures.

As a pulmonologist, I recently attended the 2021 Annual Meeting of the *American Thoracic Society (ATS),* the largest association representing health-care practitioners who treat respiratory diseases in the US. The incoming president of the *Society* gave the standard "welcoming address," which was entitled: *Can Racial And Ethnic Disparities In Respiratory Health Be Eliminated?* The talk was replete with references to the "long history of racism" in medicine, and the importance of achieving "diversity" and "equity" in health care. He was surrounded by like-minded members of the society on the podium who beamed with pride during the talk.

But the fact is that medicine is one of the least racist professions. Physicians are trained not to make distinctions when caring for the sick that are based on race, gender, or sexual preference. Beneath the skin, there are few critical variations in human anatomy and physiology between races or identity groups. Indeed, the field of medicine has traditionally been "liberal," which in the past meant *tolerant* of difference. So, to hear the president of a large medical society apologize for the "sins" of its members was disturbing. He did not offer a shred of evidence to support the thesis of his talk; instead, it was simply stated as a "fact." The talk had no real connection to medical practice; it was an example of "virtue signaling" and it was simply assumed that the entire audience shared his ideas. The possibility that some might hold a different perspective was never entertained. If it was, this group was simply ignored.

Virtually all of the subsequent talks at the conference over five days directly addressed issues of "social justice," or made it a point to allude to it. The following is a list of some of the titles of the talks:

1. *Rising Stars in Health Equity Research*
2. Mind The Gap: Ending Gender Discrimination and Sexual Harassment in Critical Care
3. Closing the Implementation Science Gap to Improve Symptom Management and Health Equity Across Critical Illness, Pulmonary and Sleep Conditions
4. Impact of Racism and Bias on Health Care Disparities
5. The Climate Gap: Connecting Equity and Sustainability to Advance Environmental Justice.

In the past, it was rare to hear such topics discussed at medical meetings, so one must question why they are suddenly so prevalent. Most attended the meeting to hear about advances in clinical medicine and basic science. But since Donald Trump's election in 2016, medicine has lost track of its primary purpose, which is to study and treat illness, and has become instead a platform for spewing Progressive ideology.

The truth is there *are* significant differences in health outcomes between the rich and the poor in society, regardless of race. According to a recent AMA study:

> Across all groups, Americans' self-reported health has declined since 1993. And race, gender and income play a bigger role in predicting health outcomes now than they did in 1993. Overall, white men in the highest income bracket were the healthiest group.

> "And actually, what's happening to the health of wealthier people is that it's remaining relatively stagnant, but the health of the lowest income group is declining substantially over time," says Frederick Zimmerman, the study's lead author and a professor at the UCLA Fielding School of Public Health. (Nelson, 2019)

The average life expectancy, a standard measure of the quality of health care, is decreasing in the US. Data show that life expectancy in the US ranks *seventh* amongst the industrialized countries of the West, an indication that America's health system needs improvement:

> Life expectancy for the US population in 2020 was 77.0 years, a decrease of 1.8 years from 2019. The age-adjusted death rate increased by 16.8 percent from 715.2 deaths per 100,000 standard population in 2019 to 835.4 in 2020. (National Vital Statistics, 2021)

Unlike what one might expect to be the case, much of the decreased life expectancy is attributable to increased mortality amongst *white* male adults.

> ...for most of the 1990s, life expectancy in the United States improved. But over the past three decades and especially after 2010, that trend has slowed among non-Hispanic whites and women, and even reversed in some places. The opioid crisis explains part of it, but not all of it, and the bad news comes amid victories in long-standing challenges: death rates from cardiovascular causes, most cancers, and HIV are all declining. (Caffrey, 2021)

The reasons for discrepancies in health delivery and outcomes are complex, but there is little evidence to suggest that they are attributable, solely, or even primarily, to some ill-defined "systemic racism" within the medical profession. Rather, poor people of *all* colors often choose, for a variety of reasons, to delay seeking health care, fail to keep scheduled appointments, ignore medical advice, and suffer from a host of environmental factors that negatively contribute to health. It may well be the case that physicians need to care more, but it is very difficult to modify patient behavior, and physicians are not trained as social workers.[7]

Certainly, the factors that contribute to healthy discrepancies merit unbiased scientific investigation. But reducing them to the fiction of "systemic racism" is dishonest. However, in the present politically correct climate, to suggest that an identity group labeled as "oppressed" might bear any responsibility for its own health outcomes is dismissed as impossible and as "racist."

According to critical race theory, which divides society into "oppressed" and "oppressors," the "oppressed" are never responsible for their actions. But this stance runs counter to traditional notions of morality and undermines the function of a healthy society. Indeed, adopting such a stance is itself "racist," as it labels the "oppressed" group as intractably inferior. In "woke" terms, the "oppressed" are beyond redemption because they must be maintained as permanently subservient to confirm the Progressive narrative.

Virtually all of the speakers at the conference found ways, at times obviously tangential or circuitous, to reference some aspect of social justice in their talks. When one observes such homogeneity of purpose and language, something must be driving it. So, why are so many of America's physicians currently responding like "lemmings" to the

---

7   In recent years, many young physicians, steeped in the "social justice" agenda of Progressivism have taken to spending hours on the phone and writing letters and e-mails for patients who have social challenges. This is a highly inefficient use of their time, especially in settings where there are social workers and other professionals better suited to carry out such tasks.

Progressive ideological "sea?" As human decision-making is rooted in self-affirming emotional factors, the question should be asked, *qui bono* (who benefits)? (Haidt, 2013)

Sigmund Freud opined that man is motivated by money, power, and love/sex. Despite what one sees on bumper stickers and lawn signs in Progressive suburbs, love is not a piece of the present culture war. As the psychoanalyst C.G. Jung noted, "Where love rules, there is no will to power; and where power predominates, love is lacking. The one is the shadow of the other" (Jung, 1949). So, common sense suggests that it may be wise to consider money and power as the logical candidates.

CHAPTER TWO: THE CORPORATE HOSPITAL

The corporations cannot commit treason, nor be outlawed nor excommunicate, for they have no souls.

—Sir Edward Coke

Corporations have always exerted a major influence on America's governance. But in recent years, their relationship to the political process has grown ever closer. In *Woke, Inc.*, entrepreneur Vivek Ramaswamy suggests that the "woke" virtue signaling of the corporate managerial class is primarily aimed at diverting attention away from the fact that wages for workers have stagnated while CEOs have greedily pursued huge profits for themselves and shareholders (Ramaswarmy, 2021). According to Ramaswamy, "there is a dysfunctional marriage between corporate America and the 'wokesters.' they hate each other but use each other for their own gain...."

Capitalism has been the major driver of innovation and individualism in America, but when unconstrained, it can be a force for societal destabilization, as it can create large disparities in wealth. That occurred in America in the late nineteenth century, during the age of the "robber barons," and it is happening again today.[8] Democratic societies tend to

---

8   Theodore Roosevelt rose to the occasion by breaking up the large monopolies under the Anti-Trust Acts. Although the idea is often raised, Congress today, corrupted by large donations, appears unwilling to follow in Roosevelt's footsteps.

fail when the benefits of capitalism are accrued by the wealthy at the expense of the middle class. Oligarchy and kleptocracy are incompatible with democracy.

Corporations tend to thrive when government policies are stable. Extreme factionalism, as we are witnessing today, thwarts legislative efficiency and leads to uncertainty due to unstable regulations that can negatively impact corporate profits. There has been a trend toward companies growing in size and seeking global markets since the 1990s. For these reasons, many corporations have increasingly viewed Chinese communist "capitalism" as a more business-friendly model of governance. The corporate shift toward favoring China represents an existential threat to American democracy and freedom.

These factors have all been exacerbated by the current pandemic. As a consequence of governmental lockdowns in response to the perceived threat many small retail stores were forced to close their doors permanently. On the other hand, large corporations and online merchants, including *Amazon, Facebook, Wal-Mart, Netflix*, etc., reaped unprecedented financial rewards. The pharmaceutical industry, with the help of the federal government, has made billions of dollars from the mass distribution of vaccines. When Joe Biden promises to vaccinate all of the citizens of the world as well, they grow even richer.

Fascism is defined as a political philosophy that favors centralized autocratic government, economic and social regimentation, and forcible suppression of opposition. The current cooperation between the Democratic Party and global corporations together with efforts to centralize authority in government, appears to be moving the US closer to a mode of neo-fascism.[9] An alarming example of fascism in a democratic country has been the recent crackdown on dissent on Canada

---

9   Elements of fascism have emerged throughout the West in its response to the pandemic, including in parts of Europe, Australia, and Canada.

promulgated by Justin Trudeau. The Biden administration encouraged the actions of our neighbor to the north and appears to be traveling on a parallel path.

But how does the American health system figure into this scenario? In the not-so-distant past, the medical profession was careful to distance itself from the appearance of financial greed or speculation. Of course, physicians were reimbursed for their services, but they avoided engaging in economic competition. But that was before hospitals began to merge to form corporations and decided that it was financially advantageous to advertise their "brand" and to actively cooperate with the private sector.

Since the early twentieth century, academic teaching hospitals have set the tone for medical practice in America. Their role has been to train physicians and research scientists and to set standards for medical care in the community. Until the end of the twentieth century, hospitals were primarily led by accomplished physicians, not by physicians with MBAs from the Ivy League. But this changed in the 1990s.

In 1994, Brigham and Women's Hospital and Massachusetts General Hospital, the largest of Harvard University's teaching hospitals, merged to form Partners Healthcare. This began a trend toward the transformation of hospital practice from a professional to a corporate model. In response to Partners, the remaining Boston hospitals scrambled to affiliate, and hospitals across the country followed suit.

The old professional model of hospital practice had not attended well to the burgeoning costs of health care, and as a result, most hospitals routinely ended the fiscal year well into the "red." As they served as "non-profits," their financial bottom-line had not been a priority. But eventually, the annual deficits proved burdensome, and imposing financial accountability seemed reasonable. But as might be expected, medicine-as-business had a different set of priorities. Although hospitals will not admit that they are businesses for fear of evoking negative reactions from the public, that is what they are. To avoid negative publicity, they emphasize the altruistic aspects of their practices, but internally, the focus is increasingly on financial health.

Like most businesses, the corporate hospital is concerned with streamlining costs and promoting efficiency. For example, in 2017, *Partners Healthcare* announced that it would cut more than $600 million in its expense budget over the ensuing three years. This initiative, termed "Partners 2.0," reduced costs in research, health-care delivery, revenue collection, and the supply chain. But in order to accomplish this, it was necessary to outsource many "non-essential" jobs to India. Like other corporations in the 1990s, large hospitals participated in the globalist strategy of off-shoring good-paying jobs to Asia.

The corporate hospital playbook evoked new expectations of its staff. Job security decreased due to competitive pressures. Economic Darwinism set in, and only the leanest hospitals were able to survive, while many smaller community hospitals were forced to close. Physicians now found themselves working for a corporation, rather than as loosely affiliated independent professional colleagues. Efficiency and productivity were now routinely monitored. For some physicians who began practicing before the 1990s, these were troubling changes, whereas younger ones tended to accept the changes, ignorant of how things used to be.

WHERE DOES THE MONEY GO?

Medicine today is big business. But that is a problem, as non-profits are not supposed to reap gains. Instead, the law requires that they re-invest any profits they may accrue back into their running budgets. Nevertheless, there are those who *do* profit in the current system. Hospital CEOs may demand salaries with seven zeroes, justifying their remuneration based on "unique" talents. As a recent article in *Forbes Magazine* notes:

> A report *Investigating The Top 82 U.S. Non-Profit Hospitals, Quantifying Government Payments and Financial Assets* looked at large nonprofits organized as charities under IRS Section 501(c)3 with the mission of delivering affordable health care to their communities. It found that these hospitals add billions of dollars annually to their bottom line, lavishly compensate CEOs, and spend millions of dollars, generated by patient fees, lobbying government to defend the status quo.
>
> Last year, patients spent one out of every seven US health-care dollars within these powerful networks. Many are household names like Mayo Clinic in Rochester, MN; Cleveland Clinic, in Cleveland, OH; and Partners Healthcare in Boston, Massachusetts. These powerful institutions are organized as public charities – not as for-profit corporations. Their mission is to deliver the latest in medical technologies and affordable health care to their communities. Any "profits" must be re-invested into their charitable mission. However, these eighty-two non-profit medical providers are making big money. Last year, their combined net assets increased from $164.2 billion to $203.1 billion—that's 23.6-percent growth. Meanwhile, their executives are highly compensated. The Banner health chief executive officer and president earned $21.6 million and their executive vice president and CEO made $12 million last year. Top executives at Memorial Hermann Health System, Kaiser Health, Ascension, Advocate Health Care, and Northwestern Memorial made between $10 million and $18 million. (Andrzejewski, 2019)

These are huge salaries by any standards, and recall that there are no stock-holders to share the wealth or decide the supposed merits of these CEOs.

Non-profit hospitals must avoid running afoul of government regulations. A hospital that fails to meet the requirements of Section 501 of the IRS code with respect to one or more of the facilities it operates can expect possible revocation of its tax-exempt status. A recent article summarizes the issue:

Let's shine the spotlight on Partners Healthcare, the conglomerate health-care entity that delivers care among Harvard hospitals in Massachusetts. The health-care system does not disclose its government-related payments, specifically those from Medicare and Medicaid. It received $25.3 million from the state and $907 million in total federal payments. The CEO of Partners raked in $4.7 million in 2016. Again, this is a non-profit company. The stated goal of *Partners Healthcare* is patient care, research, teaching, and service to the local community. The hospitals within the system treat approximately one-third of the patients in Boston. While the Partners system discloses charges, it does not disclose the actual real prices paid by patients. In fact, only fourteen of eighty-two (17 percent) of hospitals in the series disclosed the amount of revenue they derived from Medicare or Medicaid. None disclosed the actual costs. Direct, reproducible actual cost pricing is not ubiquitously available. (Menger, 2019)[10]

As non-profits, hospitals must make efforts to hide their financial activities from scrutiny, and they do this by fostering friendly ties with local government officials and with the press. For example, they may maintain a press office whose role is, in part, to foster friendly relationships with journalists, with the hope that any potential scandals will be buried far away from the front pages.

But efforts to avoid scrutiny do not always succeed. Consider the following article about Mass General Brigham, the current avatar of *Partners Healthcare*:

Mass General Brigham's proposed expansion into the suburbs would net the health system an estimated $385 million a year in profits, according to a report released Wednesday by (Massachusetts') Attorney General Maura Healey, raising questions about the expansion's impacts on overall health-care costs in the state. Healey spokesperson Jillian Fennimore said the attorney general's office has a legal mandate to monitor trends and cost drivers in the health-care market. "This report is intended to provide important information

---

10 Although I have referenced *Partners Healthcare* here, it is by no means unique with respect to what is transpiring in the health-care world but tends to receive attention because of its status.

about the potential impact of MGB's expansion projects on health-care costs," Fennimore said in a statement. "We want to encourage a robust and transparent analysis of this proposal and its impacts on health-care affordability, access, and equity." (Schoenberg, 2021)

The cat and mouse game between the corporate hospital system and government plays out daily as "non-profits" seek new ways of veiling huge profits from government examination.

THE MANAGERIAL CLASS

The hospital staff does not share profits "equitably" with the hospital's managerial leadership. In good years, the working staff may receive raises that keep up with the rate of annual inflation, whereas in other years, salaries may be frozen or a small end-of-year bonus awarded in lieu of raises. On the other hand, the hospital leadership continues to benefit financially on most years, regardless of the hospital's performance.

The loyalties of heads of the major hospital departments, e.g., the departments of medicine, surgery, psychiatry, etc., have Janus-faced roles. They are positioned between the working staff that they theoretically represent, and the higher-ups of the hospital administration, who are positioned to decide their professional fate. In the past, a department head was primarily chosen on the basis of academic accomplishment. He was considered "first amongst his peers" and charged with representing the interests of his colleagues. But today the notion of peerage is over and done, and department heads are part of the managerial class. As a consequence, the hospital staff is divided into "haves" and "have nots," and the "leadership" sets and enforces departmental policy.

Appointments to leadership positions are made by the department head, who understandably tends to surround himself with those who approve of his policies. The department chairman works closely with a financial manager, a non-physician with an MBA., whose main concerns are to maintain the department's "fiscal health" and to safeguard his well-compensated position. The important decisions concerning department policy are made by them in concert.

The hospital's managers have, like others in Progressive society, grown increasingly authoritarian and intolerant of dissent. Failure to follow the many rules imposed by leadership is certain to result in reprimand. But to maintain the impression of inclusiveness, the department head establishes multiple "committees" and tasks them with various goals. The committees meet frequently, but accomplish little, as they have no power. They report back to the department head who is as likely as not to ignore any suggestions. Instead, committee members find their days filled with non-productive administrative matters that interfere with patient care and research. The primary benefit of these positions is political, as academic advancement hinges on having done committee service.

STAFF MEETINGS

Department staff meetings have always been part of hospital routine. But in the past, attendance was optional and they were primarily devoted to topics of medical interest. Today, they are compulsory business meetings, in which flow charts and graphs demonstrating changes in administrative positions, and updates concerning the current financial state of the department, are exhibited. The administrative flow-charts are in constant flux, interpreted as evidence of "progress" by the leadership. New job titles are created, old ones decommissioned or simply re-named, all changes displayed in slick *PowerPoint* presentations.

Continuous efforts are made to bolster productivity and efficiency. These are formulated as challenges with specific goals, and incentivized by trivial salary bonuses. The staff is invariably eager to comply. The results of these efforts are monitored, and those who fail to meet expectations may be singled out as having compromised the group's success. Failure to procure a $25 bonus can evoke irate responses from colleagues.

Progress at the corporate hospital is not necessarily judged by real positive outcomes but by change itself. New hospital mission statements are regularly issued in the form of punchy quotes and logos that advertise the hospital's goals of "excellence" in clinical care and research, together with statements of "concern" for patients. But these changes rarely result in any real effect on the quality of patient care. Rather, they are examples of the hospital's "virtue signaling."[11]

Furthermore, new ideas that are put into practice often make little sense. The brainstorming of a chairman may trigger an expensive new construction project, only to see it demolished months after completion when a "better" idea arises. But it can be professionally perilous to question such absurdities, and like Hans Christian Andersen's tale of the *Emperor's New Clothes*, few are sufficiently courageous to speak out concerning what is transpiring.

At the top of the hospital's managerial food chain sits the hospital CEO, usually a physician, often with an MBA, who has given up clinical practice to assume a new well-compensated political role as a bureaucratic "visionary." He reports to the board of trustees, a small group of well-heeled elites within the community that includes heads of large law firms, financial institutions, etc. The board focuses on the hospital's finances, fund-raising, its relations with local and central governments, and promoting the hospital's reputation.

As middle management, the department head must please his corporate higher-ups if he is to advance his career, which may mean

---

11 I returned from a three-month course in Tropical Medicine with suggestions that my department consider engaging in cooperative ventures with third-world countries in Africa and Asia. The idea was greeted with enthusiasm and it resulted in a new virtuous mission statement being added to the departmental website but little else.

moving up to become dean of the medical school or president of his (or another large) hospital corporation. For this reason, he must also try to keep his department staff from filing complaints about his behavior. Should the staff become disgruntled because its needs are not being met, efforts will be made to distract them with the equivalent of ancient Rome's "bread and circus."

To this end, events are regularly scheduled to celebrate the department's accomplishments, in which the department head will enthusiastically laud what "we" have been accomplishing as a group. These are joyous occasions for self-congratulation. "Staff Member of the Month" and similar awards are accompanied by celebrations, in which pins, ribbons, ice cream, and cake, are distributed to the awardees. Plaques and photographs may be strategically placed on the hospital's walls to advertise accomplishments to staff, patients, and visitors. Such events never occurred in the past when hospital medicine was a professional endeavor. They are evidence of the influence of the corporate transformation. To commemorate my first thirty years on hospital staff, I received a small lapel pin with an engraving of the hospital's facade on it. It sits to this day at the back of one of my clothes drawers.[12] [13]

HOSPITAL BUREAUCRACY

Like those in the private sector, the size of hospital non-profit bureaucracies has increased exponentially over the last decade. An article in the *Harvard Business Review* made the following observations:

- Bureaucracy is growing.
- Bureaucracy is destroying value in innumerable ways, including slowing problem solving, discouraging innova-

---

12 In all fairness, for my fortieth year, I did receive an ice bucket with the logo of the hospital on it. I don't use it, but it was a great improvement over the lapel pin.

13 Perhaps I am ungrateful, as I have colleagues who proudly display such "awards" in their homes. They are what might be termed "company men" and that is their prerogative.

tion, and diverting huge amounts of time into politicking and "working the system."

- CEOs are substantially less likely than frontline staff to see bureaucratic barriers in their organizations. (Segel, 2017)

The expense of maintaining the medical bureaucracy is substantial. The average annual salary of a new HR manager is $70K and can range to more than twice this amount. Questionably necessary calls for new offices of diversity training, add to bureaucratic expenses. The primary role of the current medical bureaucracy is to affirm the Progressive ideas *du jour*, particularly at academic hospitals that have close university ties. Instituting policies for diversity in hires and keeping the staff abreast of the ideology-driven policies of the hospital are the prime justifications for their existence.

Staff members who are not on board with the new policies can expect to receive warnings that may culminate in dismissal, as there is no place for real dissent in the corporate system. This is very different from how the hospital functioned under the professional model, when polite differences of opinion could be voiced without fear of recrimination. Historically, medicine had been part of the liberal tradition, in which open civil discourse was valued. Today, dissenting opinions are silenced, and truth suffers.

What is perhaps most disturbing about the Progressive corporate hospital is its pseudoscientific agenda. Those who know the history of medicine recognize that it took centuries for it to establish itself as an honest purveyor of empirical science. Now, in just a short time, it has sacrificed much of its credibility in that regard, as there is no science to support many recent Progressive ideas. For example, there is no credible scientific evidence that "diversity" or "equity" promote the quality or efficiency of health-care delivery. Instead, statements like the following from St. George's University's Medical School website are made with no evidence:

> To provide the best possible care for all patients and help minimize racial disparities, medical professionals need to acknowledge and recognize differences among varying populations. Diversity among physicians—pertaining to socioeconomic status, race, gender identity, and so on—is key. Many physicians already recognize that a commitment to diversity is critical, yet there is still progress to be made.

The notion of equating an idea that may "sound good" with truth is wrong, but it carries the day in Progressive circles. Progressive ideas are deemed unassailable, as they affirm that the hospital is "virtuous" and on board with the "woke" agenda. The small number of remaining conservatives at elite academic institutions who take exception to what is transpiring now have the choice of either refraining from making objections or leaving their positions.

"Cancel culture" is operative. Like in a totalitarian police state, hospital workers are encouraged to report staff members whose behaviors somehow make them feel "uncomfortable." The criteria for their discomfort are left undefined. Instead, there is an open agenda to rid the medical system of conservative "dinosaurs," who are judged to be out of touch, reactionary, and dangerous, preferably without having to fire them outright, so as to avoid pesky lawsuits.[14] But most conservatives see the handwriting on the wall, as they are routinely singled out unfairly for punishments for imagined "rule infractions," as the hospital leadership documents a case that will justify dismissal without legal recourse. As one colleague confided to me:

> I was summoned to my chairman's office and confronted with the

---

14 This term was actually employed by a hospital administrator in a talk that suggested that the policies of the hospital were about to be transformed and that a first step would be cleaning house of conservative "dinosaurs."

accusation that I had offended a member of the support staff. When I asked about the specifics of my offense, I was told that they would not be shared. When I next asked who had made the accusation, I received the same response. Nevertheless, the remark was somehow judged to have violated "hospital policy." I was unaware that the hospital even had a "policy," having never heard it for all the time I worked there.

The scenario is "Kafkaesque."

PROGRESSIVE EDUCATION

Hospital policy must be inferred from compulsory information sessions that focus on hospital safety and standards of conduct. "Safety" is broadly defined as both physical and psychological. Language is the medium for promoting the Progressive agenda. Frequent changes in the accepted meanings of words are aimed at replacing old meanings with new ones. The old language is then denigrated while the new is declared eternal "truth." George Orwell described this strategy in his criticism of Marxist/Leninist *Newspeak*. As he notes in a lengthy appendix to *1984:*

> The purpose of *Newspeak* was not only to provide a medium of expression for the world-view and mental habits proper to the devotees of Ingsoc (English Socialism), but to make all other modes of thought impossible. (Orwell, 1949)

This is the ultimate form of censorship, as it erases not only speech but thought as well. It is nothing less than brainwashing. Consider the area of identity politics, in which "Negroes" became "Blacks," then "African-Americans," then "People of Color" and then "Blacks" again. Failure to adopt the most recent nomenclature can result in being accused of being reactionary and "racist." Changes can occur so frequently as to confuse even those who aspire to remain "politically correct."

At some hospitals, medical records no longer refer to the biological sex of a patient. However, sex is an important element in the care of patients as certain diseases are linked directly to one's sex. Physicians are encouraged to ask new patients in their practice about their "pertinent pronouns," and to use these pronouns with their patients. Consider the following table's scrabble of terms:

HE/SHE	HIM/HER	HIS/HER	HIS/HERS	HIMSELF/HERSELF
Sie	Sie	Hir	Hirs	Hirself
Ey	Em	Eir	Eirs	Eirself
Ve	Ver	Vis	Vers	Verself
Tey	Ter	Tem	Ters	Terself
E	Em	Eir	Eirs	Emself

It boggles the rational mind to think that any sane physician would choose to participate in such nonsense, but they do.

Frequent mandatory computer presentations include online exams that must be passed in order to continue to practice at the hospital. These show little grasp of a physician's reality. Consider the following multiple-choice exam question that was given followed a lengthy presentation regarding how to conduct oneself at the hospital:

Question: A staff physician encounters a patient in the hospital lobby who appears to be lost. What should he do?
- Direct her to the lobby information desk for directions.
- Begin walking her in the right direction and then instruct her on how to find her way.
- Tell her that unfortunately you can't help because you are late for an appointment.
- Escort her directly to her destination.

Although "C" would likely be the choice of most busy hospital physicians, I was sufficiently savvy to know that one must choose a "politically correct" answer. But which one? With the hope of completing the test and getting back to my job as quickly as possible, I answered "A," but the computer indicated that was the wrong answer, and it forced me to return to the beginning of the exam to re-read the lengthy introductory statement and try again, as nothing less than a perfect score was "passing." So I next chose "B," only to find that I was still incorrect. After reading the introduction, now for the third time, and through a process of elimination, I assessed that the correct answer must be "D," yet I was certain that neither myself nor anyone I knew was likely to take time out of their busy day to escort a patient to a location that might be well out of their way in a large hospital. After all, one potentially could be stopped several times a day with the same request, and according to "policy" have to serve as a tour guide. For those who answered "D" initially, I am impressed that you are (choose one) A) "woke" to the bone, B) a *very* good person, C) a dyed-in-the-wool masochistic, or D) lying.

The question had obviously been created by a well-indoctrinated "woke' member of the HR staff. It was also a good indication that the hospital management had drank the "Kool-Aid" of the Progressive Left and was now offering it as a "snack" to those who worked there. Incredulous, and frankly troubled by the "correct" answer, I tried discussing it with several of my colleagues. They laughed and were otherwise unconcerned. They simply wanted to get the correct answer and get on with their day. The possibility that this might now be the hospital's official "policy" did not trouble them in the least, which is likely why I am writing this text and they are not.

THE CUSTOMER IS ALWAYS RIGHT

The transformation of the medical profession from a relational dynamic between physician and patient to that of a corporate purveyor of health care has had profound effects. Some years ago, clinical psychologists and social workers, who were at the vanguard of Progressive ideology, ceased referring to their "patients" as such, and instead began calling them "clients," arguing that the term "patient" was pejorative, pathologizing, and one that fostered an asymmetric power dynamic, with therapist as "oppressor" and patient as "oppressed." As an article in *Psychology Today* argued:

> The term *patient* implies the language of medicine and puts the therapist in a doctor-like position in which they, and they alone, have expertise on what is best for the patient. The word portrays someone seeking help as damaged, impaired, and deficient. Psychotherapists who adopt the language of medicine put themselves in a position in which they need to diagnose the disorder affecting the patient in order to provide the right treatment. (Joseph, 2013)

Progressive concerns about the relational power discrepancies implied by the term "patient" are ill-founded. The definition of the term according to the Oxford English Dictionary is:

> A "suffering, injured, or sick person under medical treatment," from Old French *pacient* (n.), from Latin *patientem* "suffering'" In Middle English, and also anyone who suffers patiently."

While admittedly not an attractive term, it does convey something *meaningful* about what it *means* to suffer from disease.

Compare this to the term client, which is preferred by many mental health-care providers today:

> *Client* (n.), "one who lives under the patronage of another," from Anglo-French *client* (c. 1300), from Latin *clientem* (nominative *cliens*) "follower, retainer" (related to *clinare* "to incline, bend"), from *klient-*, a suffixed (active participle) form of root *klei-*"to lean." The

notion apparently is "one who leans on another for protection." In ancient Rome, a plebeian under the guardianship and protection of a patrician (who was called *patronus* in this relationship).

Frankly, it is hard to imagine a definition that better describes an "asymmetric" power dynamic, so the rationale for choosing this term appears to be rooted primarily in ignorance.

Perhaps the more accurate term for those who dislike "patient" is to refer to them for what they really are in the corporate hospital, and that is "customer":

Customer (n.) late 14c., *custumer*, "customs official, toll-gatherer;" c. 1400, "one who purchases goods or supplies, one who customarily buys from the same tradesman or guild," from Anglo-French *custumer*, Old French *coustumier*, from Medieval Latin *custumarius* "a toll-gatherer, tax-collector," literally "pertaining to a custom or customs," a contraction of Latin *consuetudinarius*, from *consuetudo* "habit, usage, practice, tradition."

To date, the medical profession has yet to adopt this term, but this is certainly how many patients are currently viewed.

Progressive psychotherapists are reticent to label anyone mentally ill, perhaps for reasons of self-protection. Indeed, they will go out of their way when billing insurance companies to refer to a patient as being "dysthymic," the Greek for "unhappy," rather than giving a specific psychiatric diagnosis. Defining "mental illness" can be challenging, as Richard McNally argues in *What is Mental Illness?* This is because culture can play a role in determining some forms of psychopathology (McNally, 2012). I have elsewhere discussed this with respect to psychosomatic (somatoform) disorders (R. Kradin, 2012). Nevertheless, there are behaviors that appear to be primarily organic and lie on the extremes of the Bell curve of normality, and these can justifiably be labeled "mental illness." These include examples of disabling anxiety, severe depression, bipolarity, obsessive-compulsive disorder, schizophrenia, and other psychoses.

In the recent past, transgenderism was judged to represent a delusional state, in which despite objective evidence, an individual *imagines* that they are a member of the opposite sex. In the psychiatric lexicon, delusion is a diagnostic feature of psychosis, which has always been judged to be a severe mental illness. But as Progressivism currently prioritizes imaginings over objective reality, a delusion that fits a preferred social narrative is dubbed subjectivity, and one is expected to accept and even celebrate it as such. But how this differs from the assertion that "I am Napoleon" or that "pigs can fly" escapes reason.

Whereas the *raison d'etre* for a hospital traditionally was to deliver the best medical care, that is now only one of its goals. Substantial energy is also expended on "keeping the customer happy." Indeed, the quiz described above may best be interpreted in that light. The primary approach to customer satisfaction has been to have healthcare providers bend over backward to be accommodating. After all, from the corporate perspective, patients have choices as to where they seek care. In this regard, corporate medicine takes its cues from the Progressive mental health field, in which "empathy" has become the guiding principle (R. Kradin, 2020). Unfortunately, "empathy" is too often misconstrued as being supportive and affirming, but that's not the actual meaning of the term. As described by the psychoanalyst Heinz Kohut, the developer of the field of "self-psychology" in the 1970s, empathy meant "vicarious introspection," which according to Kohut was beneficial in the treatment of patients with narcissistic disorders[15] (Kohut, 1971). The aim was for the therapist to intuit how a patient feels and then to "mirror" those feelings back to the patient, but not

---

15 Kohut devised a mode of psychoanalytical inquiry and treatment now referred to as self-psychology. It has become the dominant approach for depth psychologists in then approach to narcissistic psychopathology. Unfortunately, there is little evidence that it is effective, and Kohut confabulated most of the case material in his papers and texts. But it does adopt an optimistic perspective and sees the patient as having been traumatized by a lack of concern by self-centered parents. In this regard, it fits well with the current Progressive perspective on mental illness.

necessarily by affirming them as correct, if they were judged to not be in the patient's interest.

This critical distinction has largely been lost on the lay public. In their lack of psychological sophistication, they have consistently confused "empathy" with "sympathy," the latter being an asymmetric response that can devolve into condescension. But reading the emotional states of others is not the strongpoint of many physicians who often suffer from neurotic conditions that tend to limit the capacity for empathic responses, as will be discussed. Instead, what one observes in medical practice today is an outpouring of saccharine sympathy by physicians for their "customers."

Hospital rounds today exemplify this. In the past, "rounds" were a formal and serious ritual. A senior physician, accompanied by junior physicians and medical students, would arrive at a patient's bedside, and the ranking junior physician would present the findings of the case. Team members were expected to listen and to ask pertinent questions. Today, the ritual of hospital rounds is very different. For reasons unbeknownst to me, *each* member of the team—often numbering ten or more—now introduce themselves, invariably by their first name, rather than as "doctor," to the patient. It goes something like this: "Hi, I'm Brittany;" "Hi, I'm Brandon," "Hi, I'm Sally," etc. By the time they are through, fifteen minutes may have elapsed. Each member of the team somehow feels compelled to add a heartfelt expression of sympathy for the patient's condition, by adding the apology, "I'm *so* sorry that you are ill and that you must be in the hospital. It must be awful."

I do not know when or where this trite ritual first began but was incredulous when I first observed it. It is apparently their best attempt at being empathic." When I made the mistake of suggesting that patients might be more comforted if they introduced themselves as "Dr. X, Y, or Z," they were incredulous. That would mean that they had to assume a position of authority, which is too harsh apparently for the young "wokesters." Somehow, they imagine that superficial apologies make patients feel better, or convince them that the medical team truly "cares." Of course, this is simply yet another example of empty "virtue signaling," but so much of interpersonal interaction falls under this rubric today that it is impossible to separate it from sincere behavior.

Of course, expressions of concern may comfort some patients, but more likely, they leave little impression. However, the truth is that no one on the medical team is to blame for the patient's illness, so why apologize? Although I've never heard a patient complain about these expressions of sympathy, I have never asked them what they think. Undoubtedly, they are more concerned with their illness. However, I have heard elderly patients comment to the effect of "what a nice young boy or girl," when referring to their intern or resident. One might argue that is not the impression that a competent physician of any age wants to leave, as it likely does not inspire confidence. But appearing competent is no longer a high priority; instead, appearing to be kind trumps everything. I may be overly cynical on the matter, but I know that I would much prefer to know that my physician knows what he or she is doing than how to be "nice."[16]

But that is a concept that these "virtue signaling" young physicians cannot entertain. After all, it is part of the "woke" agenda to be sensitive and apologize for a host of things, e.g., slavery, American exceptionalism, etc. But as will be discussed in the last section of this text, what "woke" behavior *actually* represents is simply the excessive ritualistic politeness that is one of the neuroticisms of an obsessive-compulsive personality.

---

16 This may be the real dividing line between the Progressive "woke" and conservatives. The latter voted for Donald Trump in 2020 because he was competent; the "woke" voted for Biden because he was perceived , incorrectly I might add, as "kinder" than Trump. Unfortunately, you can't practice medicine or run a country based on kindness.

In addition to "virtue signaling" and assuaging irrational feelings of "guilt," the corporate hospital physician has other reasons to be pleasing to customers. Shortly after hospitals went corporate, they began inviting patients to comment on whether their physicians had behaved in a "courteous and polite" manner. The hospital leadership would then use these evaluations to assess, reward, and punish staff members. Curiously, patients are rarely asked if they were pleased with their health outcomes, which one would imagine might be of greatest importance to them. But the corporate hospital is convinced, based on surveys, that physician behavior is the *most* important determinant of patient satisfaction because as a recent article suggests, a "good" patient experience has been demonstrably linked to *financial* gain (Morrisey, 2012):

1. Patient satisfaction leads to "customer" loyalty.

2. A single satisfied customer can increase the number of new patient consultations. On the other hand, alienating even one customer can logarithmically reduce consultations.

3. Organizations with high customer loyalty command a higher price without losing their profit or market share.

4. Loss of a patient due to dissatisfaction can result in the loss of over $200,000 in income over the lifetime of a medical practice.

5. There is an inverse correlation between patient satisfaction rates and medical malpractice suits.

6. Hospital accreditation agencies like the International Organization for Standardization (ISO), National Accreditation Board for Hospitals (NABH), Joint Commission on Accreditation of Healthcare Organizations (JCAHO), etc., all focus on quality service issues.

For all of these reasons, the importance of customer service has not been lost on the corporate hospital.

In order to encourage feedback, patients are assured that these evaluations will remain anonymous. Unfortunately, this allows disgruntled patients to express their dissatisfaction, at times with a vengeance. Patients with truly inspired levels of vindictiveness may choose to share their vitriol on social media and various websites designed specifically for this purpose, in the hope of "canceling" the physician and/ or the hospital that they perceive to have wronged them. Such evaluations can have real negative effects on the career of a physician who is unlucky enough to encounter an unhappy "customer."

Of course, no physician should be excused for being rude to a patient, and such behavior should be discouraged and punished when appropriate. But among the diverse personalities that physicians encounter daily in their practice, there will inevitably be a small number of disgruntled characters who are mentally imbalanced and litigious. The following personal anecdote represents such a case:

> I saw a seventy-four-year-old female patient in my out-patient pulmonary clinic. She was modestly overweight but by no means "morbidly obese." A long-time heavy smoker with severe emphysema, she was anxious to undergo bariatric (weight-loss) surgery, but her surgeon first required clearance by a pulmonologist due to the severity of her lung disease. Although the operative risks from this type of surgery are not great, they are real, and due to her age and underlying condition, elective surgery could be life-threatening. As a result, I informed her that I could not in good conscience approve her surgery.

> That's when she lost it. Alternately screaming and crying, she told me that she *must* be thin because she needed to be a *new* person with an active social life, and then accused me of not wanting to help her. I assured her that was not the case, and suggested that if she quit smoking, took all of her pulmonary medications as prescribed, and

returned in a month, I would re-assess her condition, and if it were improved, I would approve the surgery. Unfortunately, when she returned, her lung function was measurably worse. When I told her that I still could not approve the surgery, she stormed out of my office, complained loudly for all to hear at the front desk, filed a complaint with the hospital, and posted a series of nasty comments about me on a social media site that are there to this day.

In the past, it was understood that unfortunate encounters of this type happen, and unless complaints were frequent or serious enough, the accused physician would likely be reassured not to worry about it. But in the age of corporate medicine, that is no longer true. Following this incident, I was asked by the department chair to explain what had transpired. When I attempted to, I was informed that there was *no* satisfactory explanation. Instead, what mattered was that there was an unhappy customer, and this could detract from the hospital's bottom-line. Concern for keeping the customer satisfied has led to an increased emphasis on monitoring the care provided by the hospital staff, and in the ersatz current *#metoo* movement, *all* patients are to be believed, whether their complaints are well-founded or not. So, where does that leave the physician who has the unfortunate experience of encountering a dissatisfied patient? The answer is out of luck.

When I became a physician, I took an oath swearing to *primum nil nocere*, i.e., "first do no harm." I took the oath seriously then and still do. Perhaps another physician would have approved her surgery, but in good faith, I could not. My decision was based on concern for her well-being, as risky elective procedures can cost lives. Indeed, as in other aspects of life, there is evidence that physician practice tends to become more conservative with time (Garber, 2019). But that is no longer the prevailing concern. Indeed, when rotating through a psychopharmacology clinic some years ago, I was told by a senior psychiatrist that my role was to give patients "what they want," even if a pharmacological intervention was not clearly warranted. Satisfying the patient's desires has become the highest priority, with arguably insufficient attention to medical consequences.

Of course, aiming at a favorable patient experience is a valid goal, but like any other, it must be contextualized. The truth is that the most competent physician—ideally what patients *should* be seeking— may not always be the most agreeable one. A crusty curmudgeon who happens to be an excellent heart surgeon is likely a better choice to perform a complex surgical procedure than an inexperienced but affable one. As a recent study suggests:

> Some studies show *no* association between patient experience and clinical outcomes, but this is not surprising. Many factors other than patient experience can influence processes and outcomes. This is part of the reason why combining patient experience measures with other measures of quality is critical to creating an overall picture of performance. (AHRQ, 2021)

EYES ON THE PRIZE

Efficiency is highly valued by the corporate hospital. A physician who is thorough but slow can be a financial liability in a busy hospital practice. So what does a typical patient visit look like today? If you have been to your physician recently, you are undoubtedly acquainted with the following scenario. As you are relating the reason for your visit, your physician is seated at his desk, with his back toward you, eyes focused on the computer monitor in front of him. As you describe your complaints, he types on his computer, pausing only occasionally to ask questions. Throughout the session, his attention is laser-focused on a computer screen. After a time, he will likely break to conduct a cursory physical examination, only to return to his computer to enter his findings, devise a treatment plan, order lab tests, and write electronic prescriptions. At the end of the session, he will smile, shake your hand, tell you that it was good to see you, and escort you to the door, so that he can meet with his next patient. Few would honestly call this a satisfying interaction. A visit to the doctor leaves most feeling short-changed; and that is because they have been. Yet, patients will shrug their shoulders and passively accept this as the new "normal."

As physician productivity is constantly monitored, those who spend more time with their patients are penalized, compared to those who keep the assembly line moving swiftly. Indeed, if when more than the usual allotted fifteen minutes per visit is spent, the physician must document the justification in order to be reimbursed by a third-party payer. How much time is a physician visit today? Studies show that the average length of an out-patient visit with a physician is approximately fifteen minutes. That is broken down as follows: the median talk time by the patient is five minutes; the percentage of time that the physician spends at his computer constitutes greater than 80 percent of the visit length. (Tai-Seale, McGuire, & Zhang, 2007) This is a far cry from a time, not so long ago, when a physician would sit across from you and interact face to face.

After all, human interactions are *supposed* to take place face to face. Under what other circumstance would one tolerate someone who turns his back to you for 80 percent of a conversation? Speaking to the back of your physician is dehumanizing, and sadly as a society, we have accepted it as an acceptable norm. We are told this is "progress." But what is "progress," when it leaves people discomforted?

A recent Gallup poll found that 67 percent of Americans were either "very dissatisfied" or "somewhat dissatisfied" with the "availability of affordable health care," and 49 percent were dissatisfied with the "quality of medical care in the nation." These numbers are higher than any time since 2008 when 72 percent were dissatisfied with access to medical care and 53 percent were dissatisfied with its quality. (Poll, 2019)

ENTER THE ELECTRONIC HEALTH RECORD (EHR)

The level of patient dissatisfaction tracks temporally with the introduction of the electronic health record (EHR), which occurred around the time of the "Great Corporate Transformation" of hospitals. Besides certain benefits that the EHR does bring to health-care delivery, its primary purpose was to insure maximum billing capacity. Indeed, if you look through the typical EHR, it is filled with large numbers of pages that have no relevance except for billing, which can make finding the relevant medical notes exceedingly difficult. Introduced in the 1990s, adoption of the HER was slow. By 2004, only 13 percent of US health-care facilities had fully implemented it. In part, this was because many physicians resisted the change, but the new technology also raised serious procedural, professional, and ethical concerns. Patients, providers, hospitals, and their lawyers, all recognized the need for policies and standards that would ensure data security.

In 2009, under the Obama administration, EHRs received a substantial boost with the *Health Information Technology for Economic and Clinical Health (HITECH) Act,* which motivated the widespread digitization of the health record by financially incentivizing its use. Why the Obama administration took a keen interest in instituting the EHR may have had more to do with centralizing control of health information than with concern for health-care delivery, but that is a hypothesis. Although in theory, the EHR is secure, it would take very little for an interested central authority to access the health information of the American public for whatever purpose they chose.

There are other problems with the EHR, as a recent review of the topic suggests:

> The transition to electronic medical records (EHRs) was supposed to improve the quality and efficiency of health care for doctors and patients alike—but these technologies get an "F" rating for

usability from health-care professionals, and may be contributing to high rates of professional burnout, according to a new Yale-led study. (Melnick, 2019)

As it allows for the storage of clinical data, including medications, lab and radiology reports, and physician notes, the EHR has improved patient care by making health information easy for other health-care providers to access and share, potentially reducing medical errors. But the pitfalls of the EHR are numerous and rarely discussed in the hospital, where they are viewed as "progress."

A recent study found that physicians spend one to two hours on EHRs and other deskwork for every hour they spend with patients, as well as an additional one to two hours daily of personal time on EHR-related activities.

As recently as ten years ago, physicians were still scribbling notes. Now, there's a ton of structured data entry, which means that physicians have to check a lot of boxes. Often this structured data does very little to improve care; instead, it's used for billing. And looking for communication from another doctor or a specific test result in a patient's chart can be like trying to find a needle in a haystack. The boxes may have been checked, but the patient's story and information have been lost in the process. (Melnick, 2019)

And there are other, arguably greater, concerns about the EHR's effects on the quality of health care. In the past, doctors were expected to take a history from a patient, read the notes of colleagues in the medical record, examine the patient, and formulate an appropriate diagnostic and prescriptive narrative. Pondering a difficult case is a challenging intellectual process, and those who do it well are generally regarded as the best physicians by their peers. Today, use of the EHR has left us with a mere echo of that process.

A major reason is the temptation for busy physicians to save time by "cutting corners;" and the EHR provides the perfect way to do this, which is by "cutting and pasting" notes from pre-existing electronic records. Unless one is the first physician to encounter a patient, the medical history, physical exam findings, and laboratory data, can *all* be "borrowed" from previous notes and records. This allows one to create a detailed and professional-appearing note with little mental engagement, and for many physicians, that is now the rule. It is not unusual to look through an EHR and see virtually the same note copied by multiple physicians. The following personal anecdote highlights the phenomenon:

> I was recently testifying in a courtroom where a patient's medical history was in question. The lawyer referred to a note in the patient's EHR and asked if I agreed with what was written. I said that I did not, as it contradicted other firm evidence in the case. The lawyer, in an effort to discredit my opinion, pointed out that the same "fact" was found in the notes of *four* different doctors. He pointedly asked, "Could they all be wrong?"

> Interestingly, the first note had an unusual and distinct grammatical construction. The subsequent notes by three different physicians all included the same error in grammar. The probability that they would all have made the same error was negligible. What had obviously occurred was that the note had been "cut and pasted" from within the EHR, and the error simply carried along.

As anyone who has used the EHR will confirm, when an error is introduced into the medical record, it is virtually assured that it will be carried along into subsequent notes, without being detected or corrected. While in theory, physicians are supposed to scour the EHR in order to delete data that is either incorrect or no longer relevant, that rarely occurs. Instead, errors are carried forward; no one questions them.

The EHR can influence physician behaviors, and the desire to cut corners can lead to behaviors that can undermine patient care.

While attending on the medical in-patient hospital service, it is the standard role of the senior physician to supervise the work of residents and interns. They are to take a history from the patient, perform a detailed physical examination, summarize their findings, and then discuss the case with their supervisor. One day, I was called to see a new patient who had recently been admitted to the hospital. When I got to the hospital floor, a detailed note had been neatly entered into the computer by the resident physician. But when we went together to examine the patient at the bedside, the age, race, and state of health were all wrong. After an initial moment of confusion, I realized that the junior physician had neither seen nor examined the patient he was meant to present. Instead, he had read a previous detailed note in the EHR, "cut and pasted" relevant pieces from it, and then advertised it as his own. To my mind, it was an egregious error that I had never before encountered in my many years of doctoring.

This could not have happened before the EHR. The incident suggests a level of deceitfulness that has crept into medical practice. The highest priority for those raised with the EHR is to get their work done as quickly as possible and to present it in a sophisticated manner that can pass muster for genuine engagement with the case. This is easy to do because notes in the EHR can be extensive due to cutting and pasting of detailed laboratory and radiology results, all of which can be done in minutes. Without paying any attention to the content of the note, one can present a compelling multipage document. As speed and efficiency are increasingly the highest priorities in the corporate hospital, thoughtfulness and quality are arguably regarded as less important than in the past.

This ruse was serious enough in my mind for me to raise it with the director of residency training, in his own right, a "woke" thirty-something. To my mind, some type of official reprimand was in order. Instead, he listened politely and then suggested that the perpetrator of the hoax was simply "busy" and that there should be "no worries," which meant that he had either failed to grasp the seriousness of the misbehavior or simply couldn't be bothered responding to it. This level of permissiveness with respect to misconduct is seen everywhere in Progressive society, including medical practice. Personal responsibility and accountability no longer count, except when those in charge decide that they do. The director of training and the resident happened to be alumni of the same elite institution, and for whatever reason, he chose to ignore the problem. He also soon after left hospital practice to work at *Google* headquarters, and the resident in question was offered a staff position as a "legacy" appointment. Lesson: elites take care of one another.

Storing sensitive patient data in the cloud—as many EHRs do—puts it at risk of being hacked. Should a technical error occur, and the electronic software does not have the information backed up, the data will be lost. As the following study showed:

> Based on data collected by the Office for Civil Rights, Department of Health and Human Services (HHS), over half of the population in the USA might have been affected by security breaches since October 2009. This study provided an analysis of the data, presenting the numbers of individuals affected in one breach and the number of breaches.

> Medical records of at least 173 million people gathered since October 2009, have been breached and might have adversely influenced over half of the population in the USA.... It takes a considerable amount of time to educate the public and it takes substantial financial resources to prevent data breaches. (Koczkodaj, Masiak, Mazurek, & al, 2019)

Hospitals and even entire national health systems—most recently Ireland's—have proven to be vulnerable to ransomware demands by criminal hackers.

But these problems pale in comparison to a larger looming threat, which is the ability of the EHR to monitor and assist in controlling the behavior of *both* physicians and patients. I encountered this recently when I attempted to access my own medical record to check on the result of a laboratory test that I had taken. I received an automatic message that logging into my medical record had been recorded, and a warning that despite being a staff physician with access to patient data, should I make further efforts to access my health record, it would result in punitive actions.

One could argue that this shows that the system works and that my records were being safeguarded from uninvited examination. But I was a staff physician with legal access to the EHR, and these were *my* records, so I could see no reason for why I should be barred from viewing them. But patients will discover that they have little recourse when pitted against the policies of a large corporate institution. On the other hand, the EHR allows central authorities, i.e., hospitals and governments, to collect and monitor information and to assess behaviors. In theory, there are safeguards, e.g., HIPAA privacy rules that bar misuse of patient data, but the truth is that they can be bypassed by anyone with computer skills who is intent on getting at the information. And there are a variety of reasons why corporations and governments might want to know your health status. For example, do you have a genetic disorder or a health problem that your employer might want to know about because it will cost him more to obtain insurance for you? Does the government wish to limit your mobility because you have chosen not to take a mandated vaccine? To imagine that one's data is safe is foolhardy.

We are living in a new world of "big data." The big tech companies have discovered that access to information is the key to both financial gain and power. In the past, the weaponization of information was only a dream of those who wanted to control others, but now it is a reality, and we are seeing people attempting to take advantage of that fact with alarming frequency in their quest to "create a better world." The potential to monitor digital records is available to those in "leadership" positions. This includes e-mails, telephone conversations, health, and financial information. Unless efforts are made to safeguard them, in the future, personal information may be used to reward or punish individuals, as it is in Communist China today (Canales, 2021). Unfortunately, many of our aged legislators do not fully comprehend the threats of the digital world and have been slow to pass legislation required to safeguard citizen privacy.

As the digital world enters, the world of paper, be it prescriptions or money, is beginning to exit. Recently, I attempted to prescribe a medicine for a patient the old-fashioned way, by writing it on a prescription pad, only to have the pharmacy reject it, as it had not been received electronically. All expressions of medical autonomy that could potentially escape digital monitoring are increasingly frowned on as "inefficient" and denied. Yet, many Progressive physicians enthusiastically favor authoritarian control of the health system.

Consider a recent effort by the CDC to monitor the vaccine status of individuals. In the current political climate, with Americans divided concerning the role of coronavirus vaccine mandates, is it wise to award control of information to non-elected politicized bureaucrats at the CDC? Shouldn't one's medical history be kept private and away from peering eyes? Can one be assured that this information will not be used to punish those who do not conform to government mandates? Having witnessed the behavior of Progressive government over the last two years of the pandemic, I am not reassured. Nevertheless, when the measure was recently deliberated by the House of Representatives, all Democrats and twenty Republicans voted in favor of it.

But why would physicians condone this loss of freedom? There are many possible reasons, but let's continue to "follow the money."

CHAPTER THREE: FOLLOW THE MONEY

I know of no country, indeed, where the love of money has taken stronger hold on the affections of men...

—Alexis de Tocqueville on Democracy in America

Hospitals must have money in order to operate—lots of it—and academic hospitals have financial needs that community hospitals do not. For one, they must pay two sets of staff. The "clinical staff" is primarily engaged in caring for patients and teaching. It is the workhorse of the hospital, and its billing helps keep the hospital afloat. The "research staff" engages in both basic and clinical research and is supported by grants from outside agencies.

One might think that all members of a given hospital staff would get on amicably. Unfortunately, that is often not the case. Instead, there is an undercurrent level of animosity that runs between the two hospital staff. Clinicians tend to resent researchers because they are under the impression that they do not work as hard, by not caring for patients. On the other hand, the researchers condescendingly view the clinical staff as intellectually inferior and not contributing to scientific progress. This can lead to bitter disagreements concerning the disbursement of wages.

Some years ago, after completing my residency, I arranged to meet with the chairman of the department that I was considering doing subspecialty training in. He was a reputed researcher in his field. When

I entered his office, I found him lying on a couch in his stockings. He didn't bother to get up. From his apparently preferred supine position, he curtly inquired why I was there. When I began to tell him of my interest in his field, he stopped me in mid-sentence and remarked, "I don't know what you want, but I don't need any more 'toads' in my department running around treating sick patients." If he had bothered to ask, I would have told him that my primary interest at the time was in doing research. Instead, I thanked him for his time, turned around, and went back out the door.[17] Needless to say, I chose another subspecialty. But this provides some sense of how these groups view each other, as well as the level of narcissistic grandiosity that one can encounter when working in academic medicine.

Hospital research comes in two varieties. Clinical researchers conduct clinical trials with new drugs and surgical interventions, whereas basic researchers engage in animal experiments or other laboratory-based studies, aimed at elucidating the mechanisms of disease. The most valued researchers arguably are those who conduct *translational* research, i.e., those who make basic research observations and then carry them into the clinic for testing.

Nevertheless, a department head must identify the salaries of his entire staff, and do recall that basic researchers generate no income from patient care. Consequently, they must seek external sources of funding. Before the 1970s, it was fairly straightforward to have a research idea and to secure funds for its conduct from grants from federal agencies like the National Institute of Health (NIH). But over time, competition for funding has become intense. Depending on the year, 10–25 percent or less of all NIH grant applicants will be funded. In 2020 for example:

---

17 In all fairness, I doubt that this behavior would fly today in the "woke" hospital. It would be considered far too "mean." And I didn't include the never-to-be-forgotten episode of once speaking to my department head while he swiveled his chair around so that his back was facing me while he continued trimming his finger nails.

- Extramural researchers submitted 36,250 applications.
- NIH funded 7,767 awards leading to a 21.4 percent success rate.
- The average award's total cost was $559,680, an increase of $11,290 or 2.1 percent from FY 2019. (NIH, 2021)

What happens should a researcher fail to procure funding? The answer depends on whether he is at the beginning of his career or is a previously established researcher. I received my first independent grant (RO1) when I was thirty-two years old after having spent one year in my mentor's laboratory. The average age today for obtaining the same grant is an unbelievable forty-five-years-old! This reflects two trends in medicine. The first is an increase in the amount of time required to achieve competitive expertise. The second, and perhaps the more important, is that due to the tendency within the culture to coddle young people, trainees no longer feel sufficiently confident to work independently until its's almost time for them to retire. Of course, this also means that senior researchers can retain trainees in their laboratories as the equivalent of "indentured servants" for a decade longer than in the past.

A young grant applicant who fails to identify funds will likely not be offered a staff appointment and may be forced to seek employment elsewhere. An established researcher may be salaried by the hospital for a grant funding cycle (~ 1 year), with the hope of eventually procuring funding. If he is sufficiently skilled to care for patients he may join the clinical staff, alternatively, he may apply for a position at another hospital or a biotech company.

Losing grants is a serious affair, as it not only affects your salary and chances of promotion but also negatively affects everyone who works for you, i.e., PhDs, nurses, laboratory technicians, etc. Consequently, identifying funds is a constant source of anxiety for the basic researcher. As most research grants last only two to four years before they must be renewed, the researcher is forced into an incessant quest for funds. Like politicians constantly seeking campaign contributions from the time they are elected in expectation of the *next* election, researchers live on a treadmill. This serves as a serious distraction from the research that one has been funded to do.

BIG PHARMA

Clinical researchers are not in a much better position. Conducting large randomized controlled clinical trials (RCTs) is expensive, and the NIH allots only a small fraction of its annual budget toward supporting this type of research. This leaves a large vacuum for funding that must be filled. Enter the pharmaceutical industry, often referred to as *Big Pharma*.

As drug companies generally have large amounts of money on hand to invest, seeking funds from them struck hospital administrators as a good solution to supporting their clinical research staff. But as one might expect, this arrangement proved problematic. In the 1980s, Arnold Relman served as editor-in-chief of the prestigious *New England Journal of Medicine* (*NEJM*). The *NEJM* is the official journal of the Massachusetts Medical Society, and it is staffed primarily by Harvard physicians. It is widely read in the US and abroad, and clinical trial results published in *NEJM* set the standards for medical practice.

Relman had served as Chairman of the Department of Medicine at the Hospital of the University of Pennsylvania, where he earned a reputation for being tough on ethical misconduct. As Editor of the *NEJM*, he had the final say as to what was published in his journal. Together with wife and co-editor Marcia Angell, a Harvard-trained pathologist, he was responsible for maintaining the quality and veracity of the high-profile research published in the *NEJM*.[18]

---

18 Although married couples working in medicine are not uncommon, one might question the wisdom of having a couple as the editor and co-editor of a major Journal.

Relman and Angell quickly recognized the problems that were arising from the partnership between academic medicine and *Big Pharma* and chose to confront them.

The NY Times summarized what transpired in Relman's 2014 obituary (Martin, 2014):

> In a provocative essay in the New England Journal on Oct. 23, 1980, Dr. Relman, the editor-in-chief, issued the clarion call that would resound through his career, assailing the American health-care system as caring more about making money than curing the sick. He called it a "new medical-industrial complex"—a deliberate analogy to President Dwight D. Eisenhower's warning about a "military-industrial complex."
>
> His targets were not the old-line drug companies and medical-equipment suppliers, but rather a new generation of health care and medical services—profit-driven hospitals and nursing homes, diagnostic laboratories, home-care services, kidney dialysis centers, and other businesses that made up a multibillion-dollar industry.
>
> "The private health-care industry is primarily interested in selling services that are profitable, but patients are interested only in services that they need," he wrote. In an editorial, *The Times* said he had "raised a timely warning."
>
> In 2012, asked how his prediction had turned out in retrospect, Dr. Relman said medical profiteering had become even worse than he could have imagined.

The effects of the unholy alliance between the hospitals and *Big Pharma* were everywhere to be seen in hospitals. Physician offices were well-stocked with drug samples that companies wanted to push. Drug representatives, purposefully chosen for being young attractive members of both sexes, roamed the hospital halls flirting with physicians, and seeking meetings with physician "influencers," i.e., those physicians whose clinical reputations could be used to persuade doctors in community practice to prescribe their drugs. Offers of funding were everywhere, as were paraphernalia of all types: pens, coffee mugs, bracelets, all featuring drug company logos, and all handed out like water. Tickets to sports events and free meals at expensive restaurants were routine offerings to physicians. Some departments, like psychiatry, whose members tend to prescribe a host of popular psychopharmacological drugs, were kept well stocked with catered food. Every day was another smorgasbord in that department. And these were just the low-level perks.

The upper echelon of what can only properly be termed "bribes" included funds to supervise new clinical drug trials, using protocols authored by the drug companies. These funds could account for the entirety of a staff member's salary and could be substantial. Although academic hospitals have salary guidelines, in practice, an entrepreneurial physician is not limited with respect to what he can earn from outside sources.

The drug companies offered "experts" opportunities to speak at national and international conferences, where speakers were routinely wined and dined; all expenses paid. Hospital conferences on virtually any topic might be supported by drug companies. In return, the drug companies would seek approval of research findings from a clinical trial prior to their being submitted for publication, as the results of a clinical trial likely determine whether a drug will receive FDA approval or not. Failure to receive approval because of a failed clinical trial was likely to cost a pharmaceutical company millions of dollars, so they were reticent to lose control of the publication process.

Seemingly, everyone was happy. Department chairs were able to pay their clinical research staff without having to dip into their own funds. Their happiness was further enhanced when *Big Pharma* offered them positions as paid "consultants." This often meant a hefty stipend for doing nothing other than adding their name to a laundry list of other well-compensated academic medical consultants.

It should have been obvious to any ethical physician that this "partnership" represented a serious conflict of interest, and at times even met standards for outright corruption. Should charges of conflict of interest be brought against an investigator or the validity of research findings questioned, the accused clinicians invariably demurred that they were somehow able to compartmentalize their funding from their objective ability to evaluate a drug that they were testing and/or peddling. Apparently, they were not acquainted with the biblical warning of Exodus 23:8: "Take no bribes, for a bribe makes you ignore something that you clearly see."

In her 2004 book, *The Truth About the Drug Companies,* Marcia Angell elucidated the scope of the problem, summarized here from a 2009 talk she gave at Harvard Medical School:(Angell, 2009)

> The boundaries between academic medicine—medical schools, teaching hospitals, and their faculty—and the pharmaceutical industry have been dissolving since the 1980s, and the important differences between their missions are becoming blurred. Medical research, education, and clinical practice have suffered as a result.

> To a remarkable extent …medical centers have become supplicants to the drug companies, deferring to them in ways that would have been unthinkable even twenty years ago. Often, academic researchers are little more than hired hands who supply human subjects and collect data according to instructions from corporate paymasters. The sponsors keep the data, analyze it, write the papers, and decide whether and when and where to submit them for publication. In multi-center trials, researchers may not even be allowed to see all of the data, an obvious impediment to science and a perversion of standard practice....

> [Drug] manufacturers typically prefer to work with academic medical centers. Doing so increases the chances of getting research published, and, more importantly, provides drug companies access to highly influential faculty physicians—referred to by the industry as

"thought leaders" or "key opinion leaders." These are the people who write textbooks and medical-journal papers, issue practice guidelines (treatment recommendations), sit on FDA and other governmental advisory panels, head professional societies, and speak at the innumerable meetings and dinners that take place every day to teach clinicians about prescription drugs.... In addition to distorting the research agenda, there is overwhelming evidence that drug-company influence biases the research itself. Industry-supported research is far more likely to be favorable to the sponsors' products than in NIH-supported research....

[I]n 2004, after the NIH National Cholesterol Education Program called for sharply lowering the acceptable levels of 'bad' cholesterol, it was revealed that eight of nine members of the panel writing the recommendations had financial ties to the makers of cholesterol-lowering drugs....

Drug companies support educational programs even within our best medical schools and teaching hospitals, and are given virtually unfettered access to young doctors to ply them with gifts and meals and promote their wares.... This is marketing masquerading as education.... But doctors do learn something from all the ostensible education they're paid to receive. Doctors and their patients come to believe that for every ailment and discontent there is a drug, even when changes in lifestyle would be more effective. And they believe that the newest, most expensive brand-name drugs are superior to older drugs or generics, even though there is seldom any evidence to that effect because sponsors don't usually compare their drugs with older drugs at equivalent doses.

Angell offered recommendations for reforming the broken system:

Medical schools that conduct clinical trials should not accept any payments from drug companies except research support, and that support should have no strings attached.

Doctors should not accept gifts from drug companies, even small ones, and they should pay for their own meetings and continuing education. Finally, academic medical centers that patent discoveries should put them in the public domain or license them inexpensively and non-exclusively. Apologists might argue that, despite its legal transgression the pharmaceutical industry is merely trying to do its primary job—furthering the interests of its investors—and sometimes it simply goes a little too far.... But doctors, medical schools, and professional organizations have no such excuse; the medical profession's only fiduciary responsibility is to patients and the public.

But in perhaps her most damning statement, Angell suggested that:

It is simply no longer possible to believe much of the clinical research that is published, or to rely on the judgment of trusted physicians or authoritative medical guidelines. I take no pleasure in this conclusion, which I reached slowly and reluctantly over my two decades as editor of *The New England Journal of Medicine.*

Richard Horton, editor of *The Lancet,* seconded Angell's opinion:

The case against science is straightforward: much of the scientific literature, perhaps half, may simply be untrue. Afflicted by studies with small sample sizes, tiny effects, invalid exploratory analyses, and flagrant conflicts of interest, together with an obsession for pursuing fashionable trends of dubious importance, science has taken a turn toward darkness. (Horton, 2015)

I will add some personal anecdotes that touch on the issue.

In the mid-1980s, a colleague and I developed a new immunological cancer therapy that received substantial publicity (R. Kradin, Lazrus, Dubinett, & al, 1989). At the time, I was a young assistant professor, and concerns were expressed that I might not yet have the gravitas to lead such a high-profile project. I was summoned by the director of the hospital, who asked whether I might have any conflicts of interest concerning the clinical trial.

I told him that I owned ~$1,000 of stock in a company that was supplying a drug used in the treatment. He nodded his head sympathetically and suggested that I meet with the chair of the Department of Medicine, which I promptly did. When asked the same question, I responded that while I did own a small amount of stock, I was willing to divest myself of it. His response at the time took me by surprise. Rather than agree with that course of action, he insisted that I *not* sell my stock because "That would set a bad precedent, and others on the hospital staff might have to do the same." A committee was swiftly assembled to debate the issue, and it arrived at the following convenient solution that everyone should keep their investments.

Shady ethical dealings are by no means limited to *Big Pharma*. Around the same time, I was approached by the President of a rival university hospital, a well-known public figure. The meeting was held in a large oak-paneled conference room with multiple attendees positioned around a long table. The president of the university proposed that I leave my current position to work at his institution. He promised a promotion and a hefty salary increase. Their plan was to open a number of clinics in the Boston suburbs that would offer the therapy to as many who could afford to pay for it as possible. The cost without insurance was in the tens of thousands of dollars. When I responded that the therapy was still experimental and that its benefits had not yet been proven, he told me not to worry about that, as they would work it out. I thought about it overnight and then politely rejected the offer. Whereas there was nothing illegal in what had transpired, to my mind the plan was unethical.

Another story. Some years later, I was conversing with two young physician trainees in my department, encouraging them to consider spending their upcoming research year working in my laboratory. They told me that their research interests lay in other areas, and we left it at that. Some months later, they approached me with the following offer. At a local bar, they had met a young female drug rep who gave them $10K in "seed money" to do whatever research they chose with it. They took the money and came to me, suggesting that I do "some kind" of research with it and that they would author the results with me. Perhaps I should have been flattered for being asked, but I was not. I informed them instead that they were supposed to be doing their *own* research at this stage in their career, and they were not in a position to "hire" me to work for them. When I discussed the matter with our department head, he told me that the young fellows had in fact been "doing their job," which in his opinion was to find money wherever they could. I disagreed. The meeting did not go well.

I would like to say that the warnings of Relman and Angell were heeded by hospitals, but they were not. After a number of high-profile scandals, they *did* become more stringent in reporting potential conflicts of interest, but primarily as a "CYA" maneuver. Low levels of corruption were cleaned up: the small gifts, free dinners, free drug samples, etc., all came to an end. But if anything, the influence of *Big Pharma* has only increased. Research and clinical trial support continue. Funds to hospitals increased in the form of gifts, consultancies, the building of research centers, etc. continue. The trend has been for academic medical centers increasingly to "partner" with *Big Pharma* and commercial biotechnology firms. And like government, a revolving door has developed, through which academic physician researchers will leave hospitals to serve in well-compensated managerial positions at pharmaceutical and biotechnology firms.

Relman would be succeeded as editor-in-chief of the *NEJM* by Jeff Drazen in 2000. Drazen, a Harvard researcher, had spent his career working hand-in-hand with *Big Pharma*, developing drugs that were marketed as agents for the treatment of asthma. As might be expected, his attitude toward *Big Pharma* was more welcoming than his predecessor's.

OPEN ACCESS PUBLISHING

Academic promotion is largely dependent on publishing one's research. My department chair in the early 1980s told me that it didn't matter how many articles a researcher published; what mattered was the quality of the research. In those days, a single high-quality publication that moved the direction of a field might be sufficient to guarantee promotion to the highest professorial rank. But that is no longer the case. Today, it is standard policy that the more one publishes, the better one's chances of promotion. If the research is high quality, all the better, but the thrust of the message is simply "more is better." Some full professors will have hundreds of publications to their credit, many written by junior researchers in their department. In many cases, the professor will have little knowledge of what is in the article.

As there is considerable competition to publish in a small number of reputable journals, like the *New England Journal of Medicine* or *Science*, researchers can find it difficult to identify a journal willing to publish their research. This has inspired a new cottage industry devoted to publishing research for a fee. As failure to publish diminishes the possibility of renewing grants or gaining promotion, some desperate researchers will choose this path, as it may be the only way to guarantee that their research will see the light of day.

But the peer-review process for these journals is not rigorous; instead, the ability to pay the required fee virtually assures publication. A recent review on the topic addresses this approach:

> ...a very high proportion of open-access journals that purport to do peer review appear to be little more than pay-to-play scams.... Finally, open access is impractical for many researchers ... Open access fees can cost several thousand dollars, and most authors simply cannot or will not pay them. (Krawczyk & Kulczycki, 2021)

In an age of "fake news," it is discomforting to know that much of what is being published likely has little merit. Unfortunately, this phenomenon is no longer limited to open-access publications but has become more frequent in what were once considered quality journals. Consider the recent scandal surrounding an article by Mehra et al, *Hydroxychloroquine or chloroquine with or without a macrolide for treatment of COVID-19: a multinational registry analysis,* published in the *Lancet* in 2020 (Mehra et al., 2020). This article purported to show that both hydroxychloroquine (HCQ) and chloroquine had no beneficial effects in the treatment of COVID-19 and that the drugs were potentially toxic. The news was greeted gleefully by those ardently opposed to the use of these drugs. But when the results of the study were questioned by critics, the *Lancet* found it necessary to withdraw the article, with the following statement by its authors (Lancet, May 2020):

> After publication of our *Lancet* article, several concerns were raised with respect to the veracity of the data and analyses conducted by *Surgisphere Corporation* and its founder and our co-author, *Sapan Desai,* in our publication. We launched an independent third-party peer review of *Surgisphere* with the consent of *Sapan Desai* to evaluate the origination of the database elements, to confirm the completeness of the database, and to replicate the analyses presented in the paper.

> Our independent peer reviewers informed us that *Surgisphere* would not transfer the full dataset, client contracts, and the full *ISO* audit report to their servers for analysis, as such transfer would violate client agreements and confidentiality requirements. As such, our reviewers were not able to conduct an independent and private peer review and therefore notified us of their withdrawal from the peer-review process.

> We always aspire to perform our research in accordance with the highest ethical and professional guidelines. We can never forget the

responsibility we have as researchers to scrupulously ensure that we rely on data sources that adhere to our high standards. Based on this development, we can no longer vouch for the veracity of the primary data sources. Due to this unfortunate development, the authors request that the paper be retracted.

We all entered this collaboration to contribute in good faith and at a time of great need during the COVID-19 pandemic. We deeply apologize to you, the editors, and the journal readership for any embarrassment or inconvenience that this may have caused.

The letter ended with the following addendum:

MRM reports personal fees from Abbott, Medtronic, Janssen, Roivant, Triple Gene, Mesoblast, Baim Institute for Clinical Research, Portola, Bayer, NupulseCV, FineHeart, and Leviticus. FR has been paid for time spent as a committee member for clinical trials, advisory boards, other forms of consulting, and lectures or presentations; these payments were made directly to the University of Zurich, and no personal payments were received in relation to these trials or other activities since 2018. Before 2018 FR reports grants and personal fees from SJM/Abbott, grants and personal fees from Servier, personal fees from Zoll, personal fees from Astra Zeneca, personal fees from Sanofi, grants and personal fees from Novartis, personal fees from Amgen, personal fees from BMS, personal fees from Pfizer, personal fees from Fresenius, personal fees from Vifor, personal fees from Roche, grants and personal fees from Bayer, personal fees from Cardiorentis, personal fees from Boehringer Ingelheim, other from Heartware, and grants from Mars. ANP declares no competing interests.

Obviously, any retraction of research raises concerns, and in this instance, the excuses offered by the authors simply do not pass muster. It is the authors' responsibility to ascertain the veracity of their data *before* submitting it for publication, not after, so a heartfelt apology is disingenuous. It also raises another concern that is increasingly encountered today, which is that the conduct of research conducted by multiple individuals at different sites is almost impossible to supervise.

Much of today's research is a multicentered effort, and as such raises concern for its veracity. Finally, the involvement of the commercial private sector is cause for unease.

It appears that the "data" published by the *Lancet* was either inaccurate or had been made up out of whole cloth. In the past, an important article published in the midst of a pandemic would have been scoured by the editors, and its contents carefully scrutinized. The editors of the *Lancet* apparently did not bother to do that until forced to. When prestigious medical journals begin publishing "fake news," it becomes impossible to know what to believe. Recall the prescient warning of the editor of the *Lancet* in 2015, "The case against science is straightforward: much of the scientific literature, perhaps half, may simply be untrue." The world is in the midst of a global information crisis that must be addressed if the credibility of science is to be safeguarded.

Should the editors of the *Lancet* have been concerned that the article in question was less than accurate? The answer is yes, as there is a *BIG* clue in the last paragraph of the authors' retraction. Their listing of financial support by *Big Pharma* is extensive. Did *Big Pharma* have reason to discredit HCQ? The answer is absolutely yes. The medical profession currently has a huge problem with its credibility, and it has exhibited little capacity or enthusiasm for dealing with it.

CHAPTER FOUR: CHINA

Red China is not the powerful nation seeking to dominate the world.
—1951 testimony to the Committee on Armed Services and
Committee on Foreign Affairs

China is by all estimates America's foremost competitor and antagonist on the world stage. It is a totalitarian dictatorship that has enslaved ethnic and religious minorities and imprisons and murders political dissidents. With the help of American tech firms, like *Google*, it monitors the behavior of its population for activities that may not be in keeping with the positions of the Chinese Communist Party (CCP).[19]

China is also the source of the current coronavirus pandemic, and despite the enormous loss of life and money that the world has suffered as a result, it has not been subjected to penalties, nor made to account for its actions. One reason is that globalist corporations are willing to accept almost any bad behavior from China, in order to maintain access to cheap labor and a marketplace for their wares. These corporations have made a cold financial calculus that America is in decline and that

---

19 Lest anyone imagine that this behavior is limited to the Communist Chinese, the surgeon general of the US in the Biden administration, Vivek Murphy, MD, has called on "Big Tech" and the social media giants to remove what they term "misinformation" from their platforms. This isn't a matter of factual errors; rather, it refers to any information that contradicts official policies emanating from Washington, DC. The latter have repeatedly been proven incorrect. It is nothing less than a call for censorship by proxy, as the US government is prohibited by the First Amendment from limiting free speech.

China will be the future dominant economic power in coming years. (Ferguson, 2011)

It is not a coincidence that the corporate American health system has adopted stances that align with those taken by other globalist corporations. Medicine is also big business, and in agreement that there are huge profits to be made in China. A recent article in the *Wire* helps to explain why health systems want to do business with the Communist Chinese Party (CCP):

> Until two years ago, people in China who wanted medical care from Brigham and Women's Hospital, an affiliate of Harvard University, had to take a 7,000-mile plane ride to Boston. That all changed in 2018, when the Boao Evergrande International Hospital opened on China's Hainan island. The facility, a Brigham partnership with one of China's biggest property developers, is focused initially on treating breast cancer. Brigham is only one of a growing group of world-renowned American hospitals planting their flags in China. They are tapping into one of the world's fastest-growing health-care markets, one that is on track to spend $2.4 trillion annually on medical services by the year 2040. (Northrop, 2021)

Over the last quarter of a century, large hospital systems have made substantial efforts to establish lucrative financial ties with the Chinese government. They rationalize this as humanitarian activity, aimed at improving health-care delivery in the once third-world nation. But they also profit enormously from their dealings with China and do so at the expense of America's economic well-being and national security.

The CCP has a long well-documented history of stealing American technology. Until recently, Chinese Communism apparently did not inspire substantial technological innovation.[20] Consequently, the CCP found it easier and more direct to "adopt" technology from the West

---

20 In *Civilization*, Ferguson notes that China was for many centuries well ahead of the West with respect to innovation, but this came to a halt when China chose not to engage with international trade. Today, the Chinese Communist Party has opened the door to capitalism, but in a limited manner. Innovation still lags behind the West but is catching up quickly.

by any means necessary, which often meant stealing it or pressuring those who wanted to do business with China to hand it over as part of the deal.

This takes place on a regular basis in the area of medical research. According to a recent report:

> The US national security community has shared a broad consensus for years about what they say is a sustained Chinese government effort to acquire, lawfully or not, a wide range of intellectual property, including medical research.
>
> In the past couple years, the Justice Department has filed charges in multiple cases involving Chinese nationals or people suspected of working for China to steal medical technology, often involving cancer research. US officials describe these efforts as taking several different forms. One is widespread and persistent hacking attempts directed at tech companies or research labs working on technology China has identified as important.
>
> US officials say a third path is *China's Thousand Talents Program.* China identifies promising research, often at a US university, then offers funding through its *Thousand Talents Program* with the expectation it will get access to the research as well. US academics are required to tell the US government if they receive such foreign funding. (Myre, 2020)

As previously noted, identifying cheap labor for the conduct of medical research is an ongoing challenge for America's research scientists, who work with limited budgets. Except for American postgraduate fellows, who are obliged to complete a year or two doing research to qualify in their specialty, all other researchers, including PhDs and technicians, must be salaried, and few grants provide sufficient funds to support this. In addition, conducting basic research is now less attractive to young American trainees than in the past. The likelihood of success is low, as most grant applications are not funded. Research also requires long hours in the laboratory, and the timing of experiments is often not amenable to taking weekends and holidays off to "spend quality time with the family."

Until the 1990s, and before women comprised a large percentage of the physician trainee workforce, basic research fellows were easily identified. But as research funding became more competitive, and female physicians needed to juggle the demands of their child care with research, research fellows tended to focus on areas that were less time-consuming. In recent years, there has been a large move to doing public health research, especially in areas related to promoting "social justice" within the health system.

The directors of basic research laboratories were forced to seek help elsewhere, and much of the gap was filled by applicants from China. As a laboratory director, I was at times inundated daily with e-mail requests from Chinese researchers seeking positions in my laboratory. Some were established medical scientists in China who came fully funded by the CCP. They had no conflicts with their time and were willing to work long hours, weekends, and holidays, a scenario that essentially amounts to voluntary "slave labor." And unlike American physicians, the Chinese were willing to do whatever was asked of them without question.

The Chinese researchers that I hired over the years were all hard workers, affable and willing to please. But for the latter reason, it was not always possible to be totally comfortable with their experimental results, as they were not always rigorous in the conduct of their experiments when not being directly supervised. Nor was it possible to get a clear idea as to how they felt about America—although I did once surprise a middle-aged Chinese researcher sitting with her feet up on her desk while reading a biography of Gregory Peck when she thought nobody was watching. The Chinese lab workers lived together in small quarters near the hospital and rarely shared their thoughts. I often wondered how they would use the experience they had gleaned from working in my laboratory.

Several recent cases suggest that the intentions of at least some Chinese researchers in the US have not been "above board." As a statement from the US Department of Justice (2021) indicates:

A Chinese research couple was charged with stealing exosome-related trade secrets concerning the research, identification, and treatment of a range of pediatric medical conditions announced Assistant Attorney General John C. Demers of National Security, US Attorney Benjamin C. Glassman for the Southern District of Ohio, Assistant Director John Brown of the Counterintelligence Division, and FBI Special Agent in Charge Todd Wickerham of the Cincinnati division.

As a 2019 US Senate investigative report entitled *Threats to the U.S. Research Enterprise: China's Talent Recruitment Plans* highlights the problem:

American taxpayers contribute over $150 billion each year to scientific research in the United States. Through entities like the National Science Foundation, the National Institutes of Health, and the Department of Energy's National Labs, taxpayers fund innovations that contribute to our national security and profoundly change the way we live. America built this successful research enterprise on certain values: reciprocity, integrity, merit-based competition, and transparency. These values foster a free exchange of ideas, encourage the most rigorous research results to flourish, and ensure that researchers receive the benefit of their intellectual capital. The open nature of research in America is manifest; we encourage our researchers and scientists to "stand on the shoulders of giants." In turn, America attracts the best and brightest. Foreign researchers and scholars travel to the United States just to participate in the advancement of science and technology. Some countries, however, seek to exploit America's openness to advance their own national interests. The most aggressive of them has been China. China primarily does this through its more than 200 talent recruitment plans—the most prominent of which is the *Thousand Talents Plan*.

Launched in 2008, the *Thousand Talents Plan* incentivizes individuals engaged in research and development in the United States to transmit the knowledge and research they gain here to China in exchange for salaries, research funding, lab space, and other incentives. China unfairly uses the American research and expertise it obtains for its own economic and military gain. In recent years, federal agencies have discovered talent recruitment plan members who downloaded sensitive electronic research files before leaving to return to China, submitted false information when applying for grant funds, and willfully failed to disclose receiving money from the Chinese government on US grant applications. This report exposes how American taxpayer-funded research has contributed to China's global rise over the last twenty years. During that time, China openly recruited US-based researchers, scientists, and experts in the public and private sector to provide China with knowledge and intellectual capital in exchange for monetary gain and other benefits. At the same time, the federal government's grant-making agencies did little to prevent this from happening, nor did the FBI and other federal agencies develop a coordinated response to mitigate the threat. These failures continue to undermine the integrity of the American research enterprise and endanger our national security.

The entanglement between America's academic research centers and China has made it virtually impossible for basic medical science to function without Chinese assistance. This may be one reason why many of America's health experts have been unwilling to criticize China for hiding information concerning the source of COVID-19, and for being less than transparent concerning the virus' mode of spread before the pandemic began in the winter of 2020. Few American medical scientists in positions of power, including those at the NIH or CDC, have been willing to admit that continued scientific collaboration with China may be harmful to America's health. Instead, Progressives chide those who raise concerns about Chinese research for being "xenophobic" and "racist."

Supply Chain

When *COVID-19* first arrived on America's shores, it quickly became evident that America was ill-prepared to deal with a large-scale health emergency. For one thing, there was a shortage of personal protective equipment (PPE). In recent years, much of this equipment has been manufactured in China. China took advantage of this shortage by selling PPE to much of the world at inflated prices, thereby managing to profit from the pandemic.

At one point in the early days of the pandemic, when tensions were growing between America and China, due to the latter's handling of the pandemic, the CCP made veiled threats that it might withhold critical drugs and equipment from the US:

> In an article in Xinhua the state-run media agency that's largely considered the mouthpiece of the party, Beijing bragged about its handling of COVID-19, a virus that originated in the city of Wuhan and has spread quickly around the world, killing nearly 5,000 people and infecting thousands more. The article also claimed that China could impose pharmaceutical export controls which would plunge America into "the mighty sea of coronavirus." (Chakraborty, 2020)

The pharmaceuticals manufactured in China include many of the medications commonly consumed in the US. An abbreviated list includes 50 percent of the world's aspirin, 70 percent of its penicillin, and 33 percent of its acetaminophen. The wisdom of continuing to rely upon a hostile competitor for America's essential medical needs should not be in doubt. But how to decouple from China without damaging the American economy represents what may be an insoluble challenge. Until now, greed appears to have trumped all other considerations. As Vladimir Lenin remarked, "The Capitalists will sell us the rope with which we will hang them."

PART II: SARS-2 CORONAVIRUS (SARS COV2 A.K.A. COVID-19)

The pandemic caused by SARS-CoV2 (COVID-19) has been the defining moment of the early twenty-first century. It has brought to light a host of issues that were previously smoldering out of public view, and it has revealed the deep-seated problems embedded in America's health system. The deleterious influences of politics and "woke" progressive ideology have undermined the credibility of the American health-care system, previously regarded as the pinnacle of medical science in the eyes of the world.

In March 2021, I was flying on an airplane for the first time since the coronavirus pandemic began in the winter of 2019/20. I treasure my quiet time and generally spend my flight time reading or listening to music, preferring to avoid conversation with passengers sitting next to me. But I could not avoid hearing the conversation of the two women seated at my side that continued for the duration of the three-hour trip. The conversation began with one saying that she felt unsafe being on the plane for fear of contracting COVID-19, despite having recently been vaccinated. The second agreed, and although she too had been vaccinated, she had made it a point to be tested for the virus before getting on the flight and planned to be tested again after it landed. She expressed her appreciation of Dr. Anthony Fauci, who had recently suggested that even following vaccination, one could *potentially* still carry the virus in one's nasal passages and *potentially* spread it to others. According to Fauci, the vaccinated should continue to be sure to wear their masks. Both women agreed; one could never be *too* safe.

Since the pandemic began, I found myself confused by many of the official policies recommended by Dr. Fauci and Dr. Birx, as they did not concur with my own clinical expertise. Every profession has its secrets—those facts, activities, etc., that only those who practice it know and that the general public is unaware of. For example, I knew that only when a vaccine is "leaky," i.e., partially effective, can vaccinated individuals continue to act as vectors for viral spread. Hadn't Fauci, the FDA, the CDC, the drug companies, and the government, reassured the public that the new vaccines were "highly effective" and that once vaccinated, individuals would no longer need to wear masks? So what was the evidence for Fauci's recommendation? After all, if the viral spread was still occurring, then the vaccines could not be as effective as he had first claimed. Any qualified physician should know that public health advice should not be based on untested hypotheses or poorly conducted studies. Rather, it should be evidence-based; and no evidence had been offered early in the pandemic that the vaccinated were still spreading disease.

In America today, even the remote possibility of contracting coronavirus, a disease that kills less than 1 percent of those who contract it, is sufficient to drive an anxious public to extreme and *unnecessary* precautions. The media, which profits from fear-mongering, and has increasingly shown disdain for the public that it is meant to serve, has consistently exaggerated the risks of contracting COVID-19 infection. Together with the Democratic Party in an election year, they were happy to sound the alarm that Americans were dying due to Donald Trump's failure to control the pandemic. But Trump was no longer President, and the public was still frightened.

I made no effort to question my fellow passengers' impressions, as I sensed that would not be possible. Fear is experienced in reaction to a *real* threat, e.g., a growling lion in your path, whereas anxiety occurs in the absence of a concrete threat. But what is the proper term for a person concerned about contracting COVID-19? The answer is that it depends on how one assesses the threat.

Indeed, my fellow passengers reminded me of the hypochondriacs that I had encountered in medical practice. Hypochondriasis is an ancient disorder, in which individuals are anxious that they are harboring a life-threatening disease (R. Kradin, 2012). No matter how many times they are reassured that they are well, they cannot exclude the possibility that their physicians have failed to identify a serious disease. They may fixate on the possibility that they might have cancer that has not yet reached the size of detection. No matter how many times they are reassured, they return with the same concern. Hypochondriasis is a severe mental disorder that has no cure. What the hypochondriac *actually* suffers from is anxiety, doubt, and obsessional thoughts.[21] [22]

Have large numbers of Americans today become hypochondriacs? Strictly speaking, the answer is no, as hypochondriacs present with the fixed idea that they *already* are suffering from a disease. But in essence, the anxiety, doubt, and obsessional concerns are the same for the individual who is excessively concerned about his risk of contracting COVID-19. No amount of reassurance suffices to make him feel secure. But a feature of this anxiety is an inability to reason properly.

---

21 Hypochondriasis is closely related to obsessive-compulsive disorder (OCD) and almost impossible to treat. Both disorders are characterized by severe anxiety that cannot be allayed.

22 Conversely, if at some point, the hypochondriac develops a real disease and physicians must not be lulled into complacency, numb by endless false alarms.

After all, why get vaccinated if it provides no security? Isn't that the point of vaccination? The answer to that may depend on whether you hold Progressive or conservative views. The Progressive may argue that the primary role of vaccination is to safeguard the public by boosting herd immunity, whereas the conservative would likely conclude that it is to safeguard the individual. But the difference is largely theoretical. At the core, everyone is primarily concerned with protecting their own health, and I doubt that my fellow passengers were concerned about herd immunity. Of course, no vaccination is 100 percent effective; modern medicine does not provide *perfect* protection and life is *never* devoid of risk. But unless you are *very* old and/or ill, the actual risk of dying from coronavirus is *very* low.

Some may argue, what about the forty-year-old man who I recently read about who died unexpectedly from COVID-19? Doesn't that mean that everyone is at risk? The answer to that is simple. Rarely, someone who appears otherwise well will succumb to COVID-19 or to the "flu" or meningitis, etc. But these are *outliers*, rare events that should not be used to justify public health policy. They carry a comparable risk to being hit by lightning. Is that reasonable justification for never going outside when it rains? Public health policy setting is not formulated based on perfection; it is meant to be "good enough."

Of course, Americans cannot be faulted completely for being excessively anxious. After all, they have heard nothing but alarming news from the mainstream media. Outlier cases such as the one described are broadcast daily on the news. In addition, the messaging from America's public health officials and from the Biden administration can be characterized as both confused and confusing. Under what previous circumstance have America's public health experts ever counseled *vaccinated* individuals to avoid contact with others for fear of spreading or contracting disease? Can anyone recall a situation when vaccines needed to be "boosted" every few months? The answer is no because there is no precedent for this, and that is because it made no sense in the past, and still makes no sense. Unless what we are being told is far from the truth.

Anxiety has erased reason. If the women on the airplane were to receive another negative PCR test for COVID-19 the day after the flight, could they not contract the virus the day after, or the day after that, etc.? Can one ever stop testing, social distancing, wearing masks, or receiving vaccines, if there is *zero*-tolerance for contracting a disease that is rarely fatal?

Or are we now as a society so "woke," i.e., so sensitive and concerned about others, that we are willing to sacrifice our livelihoods, our children's education, and the public's mental health, in order to avoid even the slightest risk of becoming infected or of infecting others? How does this differ from the extreme neurotic concerns of the hypochondriac, a disorder that is justifiably conceived by some as a limited psychosis? If this is an appropriate path for preventing the spread of COVID-19, why do we not shutdown the country every time the seasonal flu arrives, as it also kills a substantial number of people every year? Obviously, there is something wrong with the reasoning.

My fellow passengers were intelligent and articulate; one even worked in a health-related profession. But they were unable to appreciate that with their attitude, it would *never* be safe to return to even a semblance of normality. What is troubling and unprecedented in American history is, that like so many others, they were willing to trade their freedom, and the freedom of others, for false assurances of security made by either incompetent or dishonest health "experts."

Their conversation continued: "Which vaccine did you get?" One replied, " I got the J&J vaccine, and I'm glad that I didn't get one of the mRNA vaccines because they're dangerous." In the winter of 2020,

I was often asked by patients, family, and friends which vaccine was best to take. I had to confess that I had no idea, nor did I know what their long-term effects might be. That answer might not be comforting, but it was honest, and I was confident that *no one* knew the answer, and that those who claimed otherwise were being disingenuous. After all, these gene-based vaccines had never been used before, so how could anyone claim to know the answers?

But the amazing thing was that these women thought *they* knew the answer. After all, they had heard it on *CNN* or read about it on social media, and were using that "knowledge" to comfort themselves. This is akin to the magical thinking that one sees in children who imagine that certain actions, e.g., avoiding stepping on cracks in the sidewalk, will protect them from harm. But the truth was that these women knew nothing about the vaccines, and their conversation was another piece of evidence that the pandemic was being mishandled.

As I sat there listening, it occurred to me that not too long ago, this conversation could not have taken place. Until the introduction of the Internet, most people had little access to health information. They could not tell you what a virus was, let alone have argued about the relative merits of the *Pfizer, Moderna, Astra-Zeneca,* or *Johnson & Johnson* vaccines. Instead, they would have consulted their physician, who, at least in theory was trained to answer such questions. Having an "educated" public has its advantages, but it also has serious pitfalls. People today can access information without knowing whether it has been substantiated or might be incorrect. And unlike what Progressives would have you believe; the bulk of this misinformation is not coming from Donald Trump or *Fox News*. Rather, much of it is coming from our public health "experts." [23]

It is not the podcaster Joe Rogan but so-called "experts" that have been the greatest source of "misinformation" about the coronavirus, beginning with statements that the virus could not be spread through the air, that masks do and don't work, that young children are at increased risk for getting ill and dying from the virus, and that all *must* be vaccinated.[24] They were also wrong about lockdowns and wildly over-estimated the efficacy of the mRNA vaccines as greater than 95 percent protective against contracting infection. They have repeatedly failed to consider the protective effects of acquired immunity, and have ignored critical scientific data accrued in the US and other countries since the start of the pandemic.

If trained health-care professionals can't answer important questions about COVID-19, what is the likelihood that the average person can? Should we be listening to the opinions of egotistical corporate executives, like Bill Gates, who have no training in medicine? Many in the mainstream media were appalled when President Trump offered his "medical opinions" at daily televised COVID-19 information conferences, but are not in the least disturbed when non-professionals with whom they share an ideology do so. The truth is that the "informed" public knows enough to be dangerous.

Many texts are currently being published about COVID-19, and many more will undoubtedly appear in years to come. Some will include a detailed critique of the medical literature. But it is not my

---

23 The idea of introducing "fact-checkers" might improve the situation, if it were not for the fact that the fact checkers are both biased and not well-positioned to discern truth from "misinformation." This has been proven repeatedly by social media, which has increasingly acted as a mouthpiece for the Biden administration and censored the often-correct ideas of experts who do not share the administration's narrative.

24 Justice Sotomayor in remarks around the Supreme Court's deliberation of the Biden administration vaccine mandates stated that thousands of young people were becoming seriously ill with COVID-19 and required ventilators, a statistic that has no basis in fact. One must wonder about the quality of the justices when they are capable of showing such ignorance of the facts.

aim to rehash that data here. Learning to properly evaluate scientific findings is an expertise in itself, and even then, one can never be certain that findings are free of bias. It will take years for us to get an accurate picture of the COVID-19 pandemic. Instead, what follows is a tutorial concerning the biology of coronavirus infection and its treatment. It is meant to assist the reader in evaluating the many factors that have influenced the response to the current pandemic based on the experience of an informed and hopefully objective physician.

CORONAVIRUS

Viruses are microscopic infectious agents that exist on the border of life and the inanimate (R. Kradin, 2017). They are *obligate parasites*, which means that, unlike most bacteria, they are incapable of reproducing independently and must first parasitize a host cell in order to replicate. Although viruses can infect virtually any living cell, including bacteria and plant cells, the ones that concern us infect animal and human cells.

Viruses are *very* small, measured in nanometers. It would take more than 25,000,000 viral particles to occupy a square inch. As will be discussed, most viruses are small enough to pass easily through the fabric of a cloth or through a paper surgical face mask. Viruses are comprised of small amounts of genetic material, either RNA or DNA, which serve as the templates for their reproduction. Their genetic material is "packaged" in a protein structure, and SARS-CoV-2 (COVID-19) contains four major structural proteins, namely the spike (S), membrane (M), and envelope (E) proteins, which are embedded in a viral surface glycolipid envelope, and a nucleocapsid (N) protein, which is present in the ribonucleoprotein core. (Dai & Gao 2020)

Viruses must first enter a living cell in order to replicate. To this end, they have evolved surface molecules that promote their attachment to the surface of human cells, and they contain enzymes that assist in digesting the host cell membrane. Viruses that target the respiratory tract reproduce initially within lining cells, which are located from the nasopharynx to the deep portions of the lungs. COVID-19 specifically utilizes a normally present host molecule, *angiotensin-converting enzyme (ACE-R2) receptor-2*, to attach to the outer cell membrane. The cellular distribution of this receptor is not homogeneous, and it can vary at sites in the respiratory tract, between individuals, and with age.

Furin, an enzyme produced by human cells cleaves a site on the S protein and blocks the virus from binding to the ACE-R2 (L. Thomas, 2021). SARS-CoV2 contains a mutation in a *furin cleavage site*, and this allows the virus to bind at an increased level and makes it more infective. Early on in the pandemic, molecular biologists noted that the mutant furin cleavage site was not present in naturally occurring coronaviruses; it is a "gain of function" mutation, and its presence raises the likelihood statistically-speaking that genes coding for furin may have been artificially introduced into a previously harmless coronavirus. (Quay, 2021)

Once inside the cell, the virus will hijack the host's cellular machinery for the purposes of reproduction. New virions will engorge the cell, kill it, and burst out through the damaged cell membrane to begin the cycle again. Viral replication is a simple but highly effective strategy. Each time a host coughs or sneezes in an effort to expel the irritating foreign virus, large numbers of infective viral particles are dispersed into the air in an aqueous *aerosol* to be inhaled by others.

Normal breathing is not a source of large viral loads, and the virus is most effectively spread by *symptomatic* individuals. A person breathing normally in the outside air, even when infected, constitutes a minimal risk to those around him, especially when encounters are brief or at a distance, as viral particles rapidly disperse in the ambient air. The person who continues to wear a mask while walking alone outside, or while driving alone in his car, is either grossly misinformed or acting irrationally. He is not protecting himself or others from the virus, because he is at no risk to himself or to others. Such mask-wearing is either frankly neurotic or an example of "theater" and should not be held out as an example of how to behave. It is frankly disturbing to see young healthy individuals at low risk of becoming seriously ill from COVID-19 behaving in this anxious manner, but it is evidence of how anxious, perfectionistic, and compliant, many of today's youth are.

Viral particles in the air can settle onto surfaces as *fomites* to subsequently be picked up via contact with the hands of an unsuspecting host, and introduced into the respiratory track through inadvertent contact with the nose and mouth. People will likely recall the urgent emphasis placed on carefully wiping down surfaces and repeated hand washing at the start of the pandemic. Restaurants were forced to go to extraordinary lengths to reassure an anxious public by disinfecting all surfaces and by adding air-filtration systems. But the empirical data showed that fomite spread of COVID-19 was inefficient and likely accounted for at most a small fraction of infections. The initial public health emphasis on hand-washing was incorrect, yet many people continue to sanitize their hands compulsively during the day, again with the perfectionistic notion that you can never be *too safe*.[25]

Whereas it was reasonable to adopt unproven protective strategies based on theoretical possibilities in the early response to COVID-19, once information began to accumulate as to *actual* risks, advice and behavior should have been modified. But this did not occur, and it represents a profound failure on the part of the nation's public health leaders.

---

25 It is noteworthy that frequent handwashing is a common symptom of obsessive-compulsive disorder (OCD). It was made famous by the behavior of Lady Macbeth in Shakespeare's play.

Relying on theory and rationale rather than empirical evidence is not science; it is guesswork or outright duplicity. In *Civilization*, the historian Niall Ferguson correctly makes the distinction between the physical sciences and the humanistic social sciences, both of which emerged together from the eighteenth-century Enlightenment. The physical sciences are based not simply on rationality but are rooted in empirical observation and the ability to express nature's activities in mathematical terms. Most of the Enlightenment's *philosophes* were not physical scientists; rather, they were humanists, who were pleased to have qualitative notions of reason replace what they viewed as irrational religious superstition. But their findings were not necessarily rooted in observation. Instead, abstractions were judged as "science" when based on rational ideation. Secular humanism, which is what these Enlightenment thinkers engaged in, is properly termed *ideology*.

There is currently an unfortunate tendency to equate the social sciences with the physical sciences. In most of its aspects, medicine is a physical science, rooted in biology and chemistry, and it should not be confused with a field like, e.g., sociology. It took until the twentieth century for medicine to firmly align itself with the physical sciences. Prior to that, various unproven systems of thought, e.g., homeopathy and chiropractic care, were practiced alongside the currently accepted allopathic approach to medicine (Porter, 2006). The current tendency in medicine to integrate Progressive ideology into practice has no place in medical science. Most physicians do not qualify as social scientists, and they should not mistake the social sciences as legitimate areas of medical concern or investigation.[26]

---

26 The one exception may be psychotherapy, which concerns itself with human thought processes. But even psychiatry has in recent years become more engaged with biology, and most psychiatrists today are psychopharmacologists who leave the practice of psychotherapy to psychologists and social workers. Indeed, Sigmund Freud argued that psychoanalysts did not have to have medical training but were better served by an education in the liberal arts.

Medical science requires theories to be tested against observable facts. No idea, no matter how rational, qualifies as scientific fact and never trumps what can be observed. Prioritizing ideas without evidence is a common human trait, especially in an age in which left-brained analytical activities are prioritized. However, an excessive focus on thought may be rational but unreasonable, as it often is amongst obsessional neurotics. The following example emphasizes the point:

> A young healthy obsessional man refused to walk through the basement of his home for fear that he would be exposed to radon, which is a known cause of lung cancer. When confronted with the extremity of his position, he responded that if there was *any* risk, it was worth not taking. That was his rationale and he steadfastly refused to modify his behavior.

The risk of walking through a basement that might potentially have minimal amounts of radon (the house had been tested and *none* was measured) is negligible, but it is not zero. Nature rarely provides situations in which there are *no risks* versus *certain* risks; rather, there is always grey in between. Most of us will accept a reasonable degree of risk and live comfortably with it, and this qualifies as mental health. But there are no hard criteria for what is *reasonable*. Is a 10 percent risk of harm too high, 1 percent, 0.1 percent, etc.? The only rule is that risk can never be completely eliminated. That is why perfectionism is always a neurotic illusion and a major cause of anxiety and unhappiness. Unfortunately, perfectionism is increasing in society, and it may have reached an apogee amongst "woke" Progressives.

One of the major issues that have defined the current pandemic has been an unreasonable concern with death. Inspired in part by fear-mongering by so-called "health experts" and the media, this anxiety has been festering in the culture since before the pandemic. But what "woke" Progressives refuse to accept is that they cannot expect those who are not unreasonably anxious to accept the extreme safeguards that they choose to accept for themselves. The vaccinated individual who refuses to wear a flimsy mask is not displaying reckless bravado. Rather, by today's standards, he is living with what used to be considered a modicum of courage because he can be expected to be attacked as "stupid," selfish," etc. by anxious neurotics who are willing to go to any length to eliminate risk from their environment. Consequently, the "woke" resent, to the point of hatred, anyone who takes the pandemic in stride, because it suggests that it is they who are excessively fearful. Rather than admit that they are ashamed of their cowardice, they choose to blame others for making them feel uncomfortable.

When efforts at reducing risk become extreme, quality of life is invariably reduced. The anxious response is to withdraw and hide. There is an important difference between having the courage to live freely without anxiety and slavishly choosing to avoid life. No healthy society should allow itself to be held hostage to the demands of its neurotics, no matter what level of intimidation they may bring to bear.

Respiratory viruses require a *living* host. Dead hosts don't cough or sneeze or effectively spread the virus, so a virus that is highly lethal will soon die off on its own. Ultimately, a balance must be struck between the *virulence* of the virus and the defense mechanisms of the host. When this occurs, the virus becomes *endemic*, i.e., it has identified a way of co-existing with a host population. In such a scenario, the initial severe illness caused by a new virus is eventually transformed into a milder form of disease. Most coronaviruses today cause the common cold, and there is reason to believe in the future that SARS-CoV2 will be added to that list.

At the time of my writing this text, we are in the midst of a new mutated form of the infection, the omicron variant. It appears to be highly transmissible but less virulent, producing a mild upper respiratory infection, with little mortality. In addition, as a large percentage of Americans have either been vaccinated or survived the infection, we are approaching herd immunity, which means that the spread of the virus will be diminished and the pandemic should be coming to an end.

Hospitalists know that each year a number of patients die in intensive care units from complications of seasonal influenza. Most of these patients are old and have other medical conditions, but some are young and apparently healthy. Indeed, influenza is more likely to have lethal effects on the young than COVID-19. Yet, we don't hear about these cases of influenzavirus. They are not broadcast nightly on the news, and at least until now, they have not been used to shut down schools and businesses. Nor do we mandate vaccines for the general public or villainize those who choose not to receive their annual "flu" shot? Influenza has not caused us to change our voting habits to favor a particular political party. Instead, people have accepted the small risk associated with the "flu" and live with it. But should the media and government decide to exaggerate its risks in the future, this too could change.

There were experiences in the early 2000s with other novel coronaviruses, including SARS-CoV1 and MERS (Mediterranean Respiratory Virus). Happily, neither reached pandemic proportions, due to effective public health interventions. Other coronaviruses recur seasonally and cause mild respiratory infections, especially in children. To what extent some individuals may have been resistant to COVID-19, due to immunological cross-reactivity with other less virulent coronaviruses is uncertain.[27]

---

27 There is immunological cross-reactivity between COVID-19 and SARS-CoV1 as well as MERS and some endemic coronavirus infections, but how this has affected the response to COVID-19 is uncertain.

Zoonotic Infection

Coronaviruses are zoonotic infections. This means that they are normally found in non-human species in which they are endemic, i.e., the non-human species has learned to accommodate them. But in some settings, these viruses can mutate and "jump" from their animal hosts to immunologically naïve humans to cause illness. Having never encountered the mutated virus before, man may develop unconstrained immune responses to the virus, resulting in severe inflammation, tissue injury, and death.

Many human infections are initially *zoonoses*. The plague that killed more than half of Europe's population in the fourteenth century was caused by the gram-negative bacterium, *Yersinia pestis*, which infected fleas carried by rats. Rat-infested areas allowed the bacterium to mutate and "jump" to man, causing a lymph-borne illness, bubonic plague,[28] and a highly deadly airborne form of the disease, pneumonic plague. *Yersinia pestis* is one of the microbes that have been studied for possible "gain of function" research as a potential agent for bioterrorism.

Influenzavirus, which causes seasonal "flu" is endemic in birds, but it can spread to mammals, e.g., swine (hence, "swine flu"), and then from those animals to man. The "China virus," as Donald Trump often referred to COVID-19, is a misnomer, but referring to the "Wuhan virus" is not, as numerous pathogens *are* routinely named after the site where the initial outbreak was detected such as Marburg, West Nile, Zika, MERS, Lyme, and Ebola. Despite what some "politically correct" media commentators would like to suggest, it's neither xenophobic nor racist to use such terminology; it's scientific nomenclatural convention. Older Americans may recall the "Hong Kong flu" (scientific name) that

---

28 The nursery rhyme "ring around the rosey" is a description from the Middle Ages of the enlarged lymph nodes (buboes) that appeared around the neck of those dying from the plague. As it includes appropriately, "Ashes, ashes, we all fall down."

caused a pandemic in the winter of 1968–69 or will have heard of the "Spanish flu" of 1917–18. The latter was a misnomer, as the first cases were not in Spain. Instead, the first documented case was in Kansas, although the disease almost certainly originated in Asia.

Influenzavirus and SARS-CoV2 both originated in China, and this is not a coincidence. In rural China and much of Southeast Asia, humans live in close contact with fowl and farm animals, which allows a mutant virus to "jump' from birds to swine or another mammal host, and then on to man, a scenario ideally suited for the emergence of novel human viral infections. The best way to prevent this would be to change how the rural Asian population lives, but with today's emphasis on cultural pluralism, one dare not insist on this as an effective preventative intervention.

What potentially distinguishes the present SARS- CoV2 infection from other novel viral strains is the possibility that COVID-19 was created via recombinant genetic engineering in a bio-weapons research facility in Wuhan. Of course, China has denied this, as well as the possibility that the virus may have escaped from the Wuhan facility due to poor containment procedures. But avoiding full disclosure on such matters is "standard operating procedure" for the CCP. What is stunning has been the lack of interest that governments and journalists in the West have shown in getting to the truth.

If the situation in China is not addressed, the next deadly viral pandemic is likely lurking just around the corner, and it could be far worse than what we have experienced. In recent memory, we have seen several new strains of deadly influenzavirus emerge from China, the most recent being the H1N1 influenzavirus during the winter of 2008-2009. Luckily, this proved to be less virulent than expected but we were ill-prepared to deal with it should it have proved deadly. The truth is that infectious disease experts worry constantly about what might occur should a major antigenic shift occur to produce a novel strain of "bird flu." The virulent SARS-1 virus that emerged from China in 2003 was thankfully rapidly contained due to careful public health surveillance and has not recurred. Unfortunately, this same level of surveillance monitoring did not occur for COVID-19, but it should have. Instead, the virus was allowed to escape the confines of Wuhan and to travel via infected airline passengers to Europe and the United States, at which point it was too late for case-contact monitoring to limit its spread. To put the problem into perspective, the lethality of some hemorrhagic viruses, e.g., Ebola and Marburg, approaches 90 percent, and scientists in the Wuhan Virology Institute are currently working on these viruses.

CLINICAL MANIFESTATIONS OF COVID-19

Infectious diseases reflect complex interactions between the infective agent and the host. Early in the history of the COVID-19 pandemic, it became obvious that elderly people were at the greatest risk for serious illness and death. In short order, it was determined that the male sex and a variety of underlying medical conditions, including obesity, diabetes mellitus, hypertension, cardio-pulmonary conditions, pregnancy[29] , and immunodeficiency, placed individuals at risk for severe infection and death. On the other hand, it was also clear that children were at low risk of becoming infected, less likely to spread the virus, rarely became seriously ill, and when healthy, almost never died from it. It has been theorized that this may be due in part to lower expression of ACE receptors in children or the result of cross-reactive antibodies from frequent "colds," but the explanation is still uncertain. What we do know is that the observation has been repeatedly borne out in large studies of children, and it should have changed how we approached

---

29 Pregnancy is an immunodeficient state. This allows the fetus not to undergo immunological rejection while in the womb.

the disease in the pediatric population (Berenson, 2021). Instead, more than a year after these observations were made, many children are still being forced to wear masks at school.

Unfortunately, after two years of the pandemic, it is still not possible to ascertain the *true* incidence of infection or the mortality specifically due to COVID-19. This has been the result of sloppy record-keeping and to an unfortunate but avoidable tendency to ascribe deaths to COVID-19 in patients dying for other reasons with a positive COVID-19 test. Whereas it does appear that COVID-19 is more virulent than the seasonal "flu" with a higher mortality rate, it is equally clear that the vast majority of infected individuals will survive without serious sequelae. To put this in perspective, the seasonal "flu" accounts for roughly 1.8 deaths per 100, 000 in the population, and when concomitant viral pneumonia ensues, the rate rises to 15.2 per 100,000, making it the ninth most frequent cause of death in the US. This is likely roughly one-tenth of the mortality due to COVID-19. But again, the vast majority of COVID-19-related deaths occur in the very old and sick.

Viral infections occur along a *spectrum* of severity. Many infected individuals are asymptomatic. To what extent these individuals participate in spreading infection is uncertain, but most evidence suggests that it is low and that the risk of spreading infection depends on the activity of the infection, viral burden, proximity to others, etc. Most "infectious" individuals have a high-viral load and are symptomatic, spreading the virus via cough and sneezing.

SYMPTOMS AND SIGNS OF DISEASE

Symptoms of coronavirus infection, include fever, sore throat, cough, and a characteristic unusual loss of smell and taste. Mild dyspnea (shortness of breath) is common, but severe dyspnea and decreased blood oxygen levels are ominous signs of viral pneumonia. The infection produces viremia, i.e., when a virus enters and circulates in the bloodstream, leading to distribution to organs (liver, heart, kidneys, brain, etc.) outside the respiratory system, and this can result in manifold dysfunction. However, sorting out organ injury, due to viral infection versus hemodynamic changes and shock that can complicate severe pulmonary infections, can be difficult.

Death from coronavirus, when it occurs, most often results from an acute respiratory distress syndrome (ARDS). In these cases, the lungs fill with edema fluid and proteinaceous exudate due to pulmonary microvascular injury. This results in a decline in arterial blood oxygenation, and hypoxemic tissue injury to other organs. In fulminant cases, multiorgan failure, usually heart, liver, and kidneys, contribute to death. Severe cases will require assisted ventilation, but despite this, death may occur within days, as tissue injury progresses. It is almost impossible to ascertain how much of the lung injury reflects the direct cytotoxic (killing of cells) effects of the virus versus inflammation due to host immune responses.

For patients who recover, the lungs will usually revert to normal. Alternatively, in severe cases, low-grade inflammation may persist with irreversible scarring (fibrosis) that is clinically symptomatic (Galiatsatos, 2021). The pathological changes seen in the lungs of those dying from coronavirus lung injury do not appear to be unique. They are essentially indistinguishable from those that are seen in other severe cases of viral pneumonia, e.g., influenza pneumonia. However, vascular tropism, i.e., the propensity to cause targeted damage to small blood vessels has been reported and may be specific to COVID-19. A recent disturbing statistic suggests that those who have been infected with COVID-19 carry a high risk of developing subsequent cardiac disease and stroke, but this will require confirmation. (Sidik, 2022)

There have also been a number of reports suggesting long-term sequelae due to coronavirus infections, so-called *long-covid*. As noted, virtually every organ of the body can show dysfunction in patients suffering from severe disease. Prolonged recovery from viral infections is not uncommon. For patients who survive disorders that require long-term hospitalization in an intensive care setting with ventilator support, a number of long-term sequelae are common. Fatigue, shortness of breath with exercise, and "brain fog" are common complaints. But it has not been demonstrated that these symptoms are directly related to the effects of COVID-19, as opposed to treatment-related side effects, decreased organ perfusion, post-traumatic stress due to an ICU experience, anxiety, etc.

The public should be aware that academic physicians establish their careers by reporting novel medical findings. For this reason, one can expect to see an initial flurry of reports in the medical literature that claim to describe "unique" findings due to COVID-19. Unfortunately, many will not ultimately prove to be accurate, and it may take several years before the stream of newly published data can be sorted out for its veracity. Experienced conservative physicians tend to take initial reports with a grain of salt.

TREATING COVID-19

It is fair to say that no disease in recent memory has garnered as much attention as COVID-19. Multiple factors have contributed to this, but a leading explanation is a ready access to information. Millions of people read daily about COVID-19—its symptoms, its morbidity, and how best to avoid contracting it. Nevertheless, it takes medical expertise to discern the behavior of viruses, the pathologies that they cause, their epidemiology, interventions that limit viral spread, and what constitutes an effective vaccine or treatment. And as we have seen, even the so-called "experts" have been consistently wrong.[30]

THE NATURE OF SCIENCE

It has become a mantra for some in this country to insist that we "follow the science." Dr. Anthony Fauci, the head of the National Institute of Allergy and Infectious Disease (NIAID) has gone as far as to suggest that criticizing his pronouncements on COVID-19 is equivalent to criticizing science (Berenson, 2021). But that is blatantly untrue. Most of the so-called "experts" are not scientific researchers, and they may not be as well acquainted with the complex nuances of disease as one might expect or hope to be the case.

It is important to recognize that there is no such thing as "science" taken out of context. Rather, there are various fields that use the *scientific method* to address questions concerning nature, and some fields are better at doing so than others. The scientific method, as some may recall from their early education, includes conceiving a hypothesis, testing to see whether it accords with experimental observation, and then making efforts to *disprove* it. The last element may sound odd, but a hypothesis that is immune to being *disproved* is not scientific; rather, it is an example of ideology, which means that you are free to believe it even when proven not to be true. Many of the "social sciences" fall into the category of ideology, despite claims to the contrary. For example, Sigmund Freud claimed that the basic tenets of his psychoanalysis were immutable, which places it squarely in the same

---

30 The truth is that every doctor likely holds his own impression concerning disease. Despite shared facts, their interpretations can be distinct. As a pulmonologist and an immunopathologist, I recognized that my colleagues' understanding of disease processes was not the same as mine. I had the benefit of having studied the effects of viruses under the microscope, whereas their impressions were mostly from chest radiographs. It was eye-opening to see the many misimpressions that my colleagues have about disease. I would venture to say that some of the misinformation from Dr. Fauci and others reflects their limited understanding of what COVID-19 is and how the body's immune system reacts to it.

category as religion, socialism, Progressivism, conservatism, etc., i.e., with all other " *'isms'* " which are ideologies and must be distinguished from the physical sciences. This does not mean that aspects of ideology may not have predictive power, but it does mean that they are not scientific. On the other hand, the physical sciences developed by Bacon, Galileo, Newton, and others, were based on observation and the ability to describe phenomena in mathematical terms. When an observation in nature is not adequately explained by a given scientific paradigm, a search must be initiated for a better explanation.

Those post-deconstructionist academics who claim that there is no truth, or that history is all about how one frames facts, are peddling pseudoscientific ideology. Those who create narratives out of whole cloth, or argue that 2+2 can equal 5 when it serves a societal goal are peddling Marxism with the purpose of undermining the existing system. What can be said with clarity is that scientists, including physicians, must never allow such ideologies to infiltrate and influence their practice.

THE LIMITS OF MEDICAL SCIENCE

Physics can address certain questions about the natural world with a high degree of precision. Many experiments in physics can be conducted in laboratories where conditions can be tightly controlled and repeated many times. Unfortunately, medical experiments rarely achieve such rigor. For example, when testing the effects of a new drug or vaccine, one must examine large numbers of subjects under conditions that cannot be tightly controlled. Unlike identical molecules in a flask, individuals are complex and diverse, and as such, their responses to a drug or a vaccine can be expected to vary. Repeating large-scale medical experiments with different cohorts of subjects virtually never yields the same—or necessarily even close to the same—results (R.

Kradin, 2008). Instead, one tends to identify trends in the data. For that reason, it can take considerable time for a new observation in medicine to be accepted as "truth." To suggest that it is easier to send a man to the moon than to determine how effective a new vaccine may be in a given individual may not be an overstatement. But when faced with an existential threat like a pandemic, people naturally find it hard to accept that answers may not be rapidly forthcoming.

Complicating the limits of medical science is a cultural environment in which it has become increasingly difficult to debate truth (McIntyre, 2015). Today, scientists, politicians, the media, appear to have lost track of what objective truth is, and some post-modern academics deny that it exists at all (Frankfurt, 2006). Others simply lack sufficient conscience to concern themselves with the deleterious effects that unmitigated lying has on society (Keyes, 2016). In the past, such individuals were labeled as sociopaths. Today, they may simply be your elected leader, your doctor, lawyer, teacher, or neighbor, which is to say, dishonesty is becoming normalized.

The unmitigated quest for fame, riches, and power currently allows too many people in positions of responsibility to ignore that they have an obligation to the truth. This has bred a well-deserved skepticism amongst the public that consequently doubts what it is being told. The inability to agree upon shared truths can eventually prove fatal to society, as it leads to its fragmentation. Cultures reflect shared values that bind people together in a common cause. That vital cohesion is no longer the case in America.

We are witnessing this today with respect to the information being offered regarding how best to manage the current coronavirus pandemic. Untruths, half-truths, and unproven claims have been made and used to fashion national and global health policies. Patients can unfortunately no longer be confident that they are receiving sound advice from their physicians, as the latter also rely on the information provided to them by the nation's health experts.

Many questions that should have been addressed early in the current pandemic were left unanswered. These include the actual mortality rate due to COVID-19, the risks of re-infection for those with acquired immunity after being infected with COVID-19, the true efficacy of the current vaccines with respect to protecting against infection and reducing mortality, and the complications associated with these untested vaccines. I can recall no time in recent history when access to such straightforward questions has been so difficult to identify.

The uncomfortable truth is that America's public health "experts," i.e., those designated to speak on behalf of the American government, may not be qualified to evaluate information properly or know how to use it effectively in the management of the current pandemic. This is not to suggest that the present health experts are non-intelligent but may strictly speaking, not be scientific in their approach. There is a political class within the field of medicine, and these physician bureaucrats are not necessarily rigorous scientists. When Dr. Scott Atlas, who has spent much of his career evaluating health strategies at Stanford Medical Center joined the Coronavirus Task Force and criticized lockdowns based on data showing their ineffectiveness, he met with resistance from Dr. Fauci and Dr. Birx, as well as the media. (S Atlas, 2021)

When Dr. Fauci repeatedly provides the public with muddled answers to straightforward questions or reverses himself with no explanation, the truth may be that he is not truly qualified to interpret the science of the pandemic, despite his many years of leadership at the NIH. Despite claims to the contrary, Fauci undoubtedly is more expert at medical administration than either research or medical practices. He has never personally cared for a patient with COVID-19 and almost certainly would not know how to do so, having been far removed from the day-to-day activities of hospital practice for years. This was the opinion of Dr. Kary Mullis, who received the Noble Prize for Chemistry for the development of the widely used polymerase chain reaction (PCR), back in 1993. According to Mullis:

> Guys like Fauci get up there and start talking and you know he doesn't know anything really about anything, and I'd say that to his face. The man thinks that you can take a blood sample and stick it in an electron microscope and if it's got a virus in there, you'll know it. He doesn't understand electron microscopy, and he doesn't understand medicine. And he should not be in a position like the one that he is in. Most of those guys up there are just administrative people and they don't know anything about what is going on at the bottom.... They make up their own rules as they go; they change them when they want to ...(Kennedy Jr., 2021)

I am peripherally acquainted with Dr. Fauci but well acquainted with his reputation in academic medicine circles as a politician. I have observed medical "politicians" in leadership positions all of my professional life and can confidently say that whatever their interests and talents might have been early in their careers, administrative concerns have removed the vast majority of them from hands-on knowledge of research and medical practice. That is not a criticism, except that it is wrong to pose as a medical expert in an area when one is no longer qualified to do so. Nevertheless, these are the people routinely called upon by politicians to formulate policy in public health emergencies. Consequently, the public health response is prone to being ill-conceived and poorly executed, as it has unquestionably been in the current pandemic.

The public health response to the pandemic has been based on viral testing, social distancing, the use of masks, vaccines, and therapeutics. Unfortunately, the approach to all of these has been poorly conceived and executed, leading to increased anxieties rather than confidence.

TESTING

The first step in determining the incidence (new cases) and prevalence (the total number of cases in a given population) of coronavirus is to identify the virus. To be practical, tests for COVID-19 must be both sensitive, i.e., not prone to "false" negatives, and specific, i.e., not prone to "false" positives. Unlike bacteria and fungi, isolating viruses in culture is a time-consuming technique. For this reason, mass testing generally adopts immunological techniques that identify specific viral antigens by detecting viral genetic material with techniques that amplify their presence. The polymerase chain reaction (PCR) is currently the most sensitive and specific mode of testing for COVID-19. It requires sampling from nasal swabs or directly from respiratory secretions where the viral load is likely to be high.

PCR is a remarkable and highly sensitive technology that can greatly amplify small numbers of copies of viral mRNA. It does this through repetitive cycles that exponentially increase viral DNA copy number. Due to the sensitivity of the test, very small amounts of viral mRNA messages can be detected. But cycle numbers greater than 24 tend to detect non-viable virions and will exaggerate the prevalence of infection, yielding the equivalent of "false" positives, so it is important to choose an optimal PCR cycle number and to standardize its use in testing. Unfortunately, this has not happened routinely, and it has almost certainly resulted in an overestimation of the number of individuals in the population with viable COVID-19 infection. (AACC, 2020)

Like any laboratory test, PCR includes both false positives and negatives, and this varies with the testing equipment and experience of the technical support staff. For most large-scale testing, the only answer that one gets is either *positive or negative* for the virus. But it is difficult to know exactly what a positive test means in a healthy asymptomatic individual, either with respect to their risk of developing a symptomatic disease or of spreading the infection to others.

For this reason, testing should be carried out intelligently with a definite goal in mind. As a practical matter, it may be argued that testing should have been limited to symptomatic individuals. Testing everyone is important for contact tracing when a possibility remains of limiting community spread, or as a research project designed to determine the true prevalence of infection. The non-discriminant use of population PCR testing has done little except to increase public anxiety.

With little supportive data, for most of the pandemic the CDC's advice for anyone testing positive for COVID-19, symptomatic or not, was to quarantine for fourteen days. The basis for this decision was that a small number of patients exposed to COVID-19 might develop symptoms as late as two weeks after exposure. But this is not a sound public health strategy, as the vast majority of infected individuals who become symptomatic do so within seventy-two hours. It is not rational or effective to quarantine asymptomatic individuals for two weeks because of the very small risk of their becoming symptomatic at a later date. In December of 2021, Dr. Walensky, the current head of the CDC, announced that people who test positive need only quarantine for five days, but she was unable to offer any scientific rationale for that change. Is there reliable data to suggest that asymptomatic individuals are contributing significantly to the numbers of new *symptomatic* cases in the population? The answer is *no,* but that may be due to the failure of the CDC to release the data that they have accrued concerning the pandemic. As a recent *N.Y. Times* article suggests:

> For more than a year, the Centers for Disease Control and Prevention has collected data on hospitalizations for COVID-19 in the United States and broken it down by age, race, and vaccination status. But it has not made most of the information public.

When the CDC published the first significant data on the effectiveness of boosters in adults younger than sixty-five two weeks ago, it left out the numbers for a huge portion of that population: 18–49-year-olds, the group least likely to benefit from extra shots, because the first two doses already left them well-protected. (Mandavilli, 2022)

The CDC offered no credible reason for withholding data. But the evidence would suggest that it is because that data does not support their agenda of vaccinating the entire population regardless of age or previous COVID-19 infection. But this strategy effectively bars other researchers from critically evaluating public health policy and is antithetical to the importance of transparency when conducting scientific research.

The only justification for testing asymptomatic individuals is with the intention of accepting *no level of risk,* and that makes little sense in an active pandemic. At no other time in medical history have public health experts made decisions based on tolerating *zero* risk for a disease that carries a relatively low mortality rate and can no longer be fully contained.[31]

Extreme aversion to risk has characterized the response to the COVID-19 pandemic. Experienced voices, who understand the nature of disease and can evaluate *risk: benefit* ratios have agreed that the response to the pandemic has been excessive. Unfortunately, they have been silenced by *ad hominem* attacks by an anxious public and those with a political agenda, who have accused them of being "unconcerned" about the health of others or "racist" because they are not adequately considering the effects on the black community, etc. Unfortunately, a substantial part of society is susceptible to the fear-mongering by the media, Dr. Fauci, and the Biden administration.

---

31 How deadly a disease is matters. For a disease like Ebola that kills 40–90 percent of those infected, a different strategy would be in order. But our health experts have shown no inclination to stratify their response to COVID-19 based on actual risks.

ANTIBODY TESTING

The host immune response can be divided into two arms. One mode of host immune response is termed *humoral immunity*, which reflects the ability of infected or vaccinated individuals to mount an effective antibody response to the virus. Infection with COVID-19 initiates an immune response that produces antibodies against specific viral antigens such as the nucleocapsid protein and the spike (S) protein. Specific anti-S protein antibodies target the virus's spike S1 protein and its receptor-binding domain (RBD). Serologic tests can detect the presence of these antibodies in serum days to weeks following acute infection. Serologic tests can also identify persons with resolving or past COVID-19 infection and thereby help scientists and public health experts better understand how widespread the infection has been and which populations are at increased risk of infection.

In most humoral responses, the early humoral reaction occurs within seventy-two hours and includes primarily IgM antibodies that loosely bind to viral particles. This is followed by the production of high-avidity (tightly binding) IgG antibodies. Some of these antibodies are neutralizing, which means that they can eliminate the virus or abrogate its activities. This is the effect that vaccines aim at achieving. Following infection with the coronaviruses SARS-1 and MERS, neutralizing antibodies have persisted for several years.

For respiratory coronaviruses, the presence of antibodies does not necessarily confer long-term immunity, as these viruses tend to undergo spontaneous mutations that alter their immunogenicity. But mutation does not necessarily equate to either greater infectivity or virulence of the virus. A new public health scare has emerged due to the omicron (ð) variant of COVID-19, which shows dense mutations from the native coronavirus, many in the antigenic S protein that is specifically targeted by the vaccines. The omicron variant appears to be highly contagious but not especially virulent. Consequently, its emergence should not evoke a knee-jerk public health response to limit its spread. But it has. Optimally, one should wait for data to determine how the population is responding before mandating extreme public actions. And the only data that calls for such action are large numbers of deaths or severe cases requiring hospitalization. Herculean efforts to eliminate asymptomatic or mild infections are not sound public health strategy.[32]

Although evidence of neutralizing antibody titers against COVID-19 and its variants suggest immunity, such testing is not performed routinely. Instead, the public health experts have insisted on vaccinating everyone, which is also not sound medical policy. For other types of vaccinations, e.g., hepatitis B, individuals are first tested to see if they may already be immune, and when they are, they are not vaccinated. Vaccine mandates that purposefully ignore the underlying immune status of the individual are not based in sound science.

The normal immune system has a variety of mechanisms for eliminating viruses. Cell-mediated immunity refers to the actions of cytotoxic T-lymphocytes and natural killer (NK) cells, both of which normally play an important role in limiting viral spread within the body. Unfortunately, we don't have good standardized tests to assess specific cell-mediated immunity against the coronavirus, so clinicians rely primarily on antibody levels as evidence for protective immunity. However, this ignores what is likely the primary mode of immunity to COVID-19.

---

32 Recently, the state of Florida, whose Republican Governor Ron DeSantis has been roundly criticized by the Biden administration as being glib about the virus, has called for a cessation of testing except for individuals who are ill. Although this is sound policy, it has met with widespread criticism from the Progressive media.

NATURAL IMMUNITY

What has been termed "natural immunity" in the media is more accurately termed "acquired immunity," which means that an individual has previously been infected with the virus, survived the insult, and now has acquired immunity to subsequent infection, due to circulating antibodies in the blood, B-cell precursors that can recall the viral antigen and produce new antibodies, as well as T-cell mediated immunity, which includes "memory T-cells" that can also recognize viral antigens when re-challenged. One of the advantages of "natural immunity" is that the immune system is primed not by a single or small number of viral antigens, which is the case for vaccines, but by a panoply of virus-related antigens.

Researchers at Johns Hopkins Medical Center conducted a large study of natural (acquired) immunity and showed that antibody levels against COVID-19 remained higher, and for a longer period of time, in people who had been infected by the virus, than for those who received mRNA vaccines against COVID-19 (Zhong, Xiao, Debes, & al, 2021). A widely cited study from Israel showed that natural immunity offered better protection against the delta (d) variant of the pandemic coronavirus than did two doses of the Pfizer-BioNTech mRNA vaccine. The newly released data show that people who had a COVID-19 infection were much less likely than never-infected, vaccinated people to be infected with the *delta* variant, to develop symptoms, or to be hospitalized with serious COVID-19. (Wadman, 2021) The study found that vaccinated subjects had a thirteen-fold increased risk for breakthrough infection with the delta variant compared to those naturally infected.

In the Israeli study, comparing more than 32,000 people in the health system, the risk of developing symptomatic COVID-19 was twenty-seven times higher among the vaccinated, and the risk of hospitalization eight-times higher, the opposite of what might be hoped for from an effective vaccine. With time, however, the rates of infection fell amongst the vaccinated group. Such paradoxical findings are commonly seen in controlled trials, and the data may appear to defy rational explanation. But that hasn't kept "experts" from assigning explanations to what may well be unexplainable based on our current state of knowledge. When interpretations go beyond the data, they are expressions of ideology.

Unfortunately, the US government's response to these studies has been to ignore their implications and to instead insist that vaccination is the only strategy for protecting against COVID-19, providing *no* rationale to support that stance. In general, vaccinations are contraindicated when an individual is known to have already contracted and recovered from a disease. The immune system is a complex network of interacting cells—far too complicated to impose a linear approach onto, i.e., more is not necessarily better in such a system. It does not follow that repeated vaccines that boost antibody levels are safe. One does not necessarily benefit from a revved-up immune system, as this can lead to undesirable autoimmune responses. This is why it may be unwise to continue to administer "boosters" of the original vaccines. When a new variant emerges, a vaccine that specifically targets it *may* be indicated, as it is each year with the annually mutating influenzavirus. Repeatedly administering a vaccine that has been demonstrated to be ineffective makes little sense.

Masks for Preventing the Spread of COVID-19

One of the most controversial areas with respect to the current public health approach to the pandemic has been the widespread use of population masking. The rationale for masking is spurious. Masks were introduced as public health policy primarily to limit the spread of tuberculosis, a much larger organism (0.3-0.5 micron) than a virus (~0.06 microns). People infected with COVID-19 emit viral particles when breathing, talking, yelling, coughing, sneezing, and singing. Each of these activities produces different amounts and sizes of respiratory particles. Large respiratory droplets can travel up to 6 feet before falling to the ground due to gravity. However, small aerosolized particles can be suspended in air flows and move through space to infect people at a distance. Evidence indicates that COVID-19 is most effectively transmitted in closed, indoor spaces, with limited ventilation, a scenario fostered by lockdowns. Outdoors, viral particles are prone to disperse, thereby decreasing the risk of transmitting infection.

To what extent do masks prevent the spread of COVID-19? First, it should be appreciated that all masks are not equal. The pore size of a mask determines whether it can block the entry or exit of viral particles. Due to the small size of COVID-19 and the fact that it is spread primarily as an aerosol and not by droplets, the masks worn by most of the public provide little to no protection from virus spread by others. It may help to reduce the amount of virus spread by coughing and sneezing by the mask-wearer, but actively infected individuals will likely quarantine themselves. To say that masks are totally useless *may* be an overstatement, but to conclude that they provide effective protection from contracting disease or spreading infection is unquestionably incorrect. The bottom-line is that there is no convincing scientific evidence that masks have provided any measurable benefit in reducing the spread of viral infection. (Jefferson & Jones, 2020)

One of the curious aspects of the public health response to the wearing of masks was the initial response by the CDC, the US Surgeon-General, and the COVID-19 Response Team headed by Dr. Fauci. In the early days of the pandemic, there was a legitimate concern that there might not be sufficient personal protective equipment (PPE) to supply both the hospital systems and the general public. The initial official public health advice to the public was to 1) avoid wearing masks, 2) that masks were not adequate to prevent infection, and 3) that they might increase the risk of contracting COVID-19, as people tended to inadvertently touch their faces to adjust their masks.

Masks other than N-95 masks routinely worn by medical staff are unlikely to serve as effective barriers. The N-95 filters out particles greater than 0.3 microns. This is larger than the virus but in the range that can reduce virus carried by an aqueous aerosol. But N-95 masks must be appropriately fitted and tested, and men who sport facial hair can be difficult to fit.

The official message from government health officials changed with respect to mask-wearing when they insisted that masks were protective and that wearing them should be mandatory. The Surgeon-General admitted that although his initial message may have been confusing, masking was now indeed a good thing. Fauci doubled down on the importance of masks without clarifying his initial statements or providing a rationale for their widespread use. It was widely construed that health officials were initially trying to ensure that medical personnel would have access to PPE when the pandemic first began, at a time when supply was limited. But the official advice about mask-wearing has been almost impossible to comprehend. For example, in the absence of supporting data, Dr. Redfield, the former head of the CDC under Trump, made the following hyperbolic and incorrect statement before a Senate Subcommittee in September of 2020 :

I might even go so far as to say that this face mask is more guaranteed to protect me against COVID than when I take a COVID vaccine because the immunogenicity may be 70 percent. And if I don't get an immune response, the vaccine is not going to protect me. This face mask will.

Adm. Brett Giroir, assistant secretary at Health and Human Services, testified that wearing a face-covering "is one of the most important things we can do to prevent spread," again with no supportive evidence. In January 2022, Dr. Walensky of the CDC admitted that masks other than the N-95 were ineffective at blocking the transmission of virus, but the message was not a strong one, and many continued to wear flimsy cloth and paper masks despite the scientific evidence. Now that the pandemic is likely winding down, the Biden administration claimed that it was making efforts to distribute N95 masks to the public, but this has yet to occur. At any rate, this token effort is unlikely to have any beneficial effect.

DETRIMENTAL EFFECTS OF MASKS

Mask-wearing for prolonged periods can have detrimental effects. Anyone who has worn an N-95 mask will attest to the fact that it is uncomfortable, hot, and makes normal breathing difficult. A well-fitted mask serves as a barrier not only to particles but also serves as a resistance to normal ventilation, which means that the amount of oxygen taken into the lung will fall as carbon dioxide levels rise. Over time, the latter leads to *respiratory acidosis* with abnormal acidification of the blood, cognitive deficits, headache, ventilatory depression, and brain swelling (Williams, Krah, & al, 2020). In those with underlying chronic lung disease, e.g., COPD, these effects can be life-threatening.

The long-term effects on children of being taught in classrooms without the benefit of seeing the facial expressions of teachers and fellow students are likely substantial, and research into this important topic is necessary. But *any* detrimental effects, when weighed against an intervention that is not necessary and does not work, should have been judged as unacceptable. The harm that has been done to children in the present pandemic due to the selfish concerns of anxious adults is condemnable, and it will undoubtedly be a subject of considerable interest well into the future.

The government has consistently underrated the ability of the public to comprehend facts and to accept hard truths. Ultimately, the wearing of masks became a political football with Progressive Democrats, and many top public health officials, the nation's academic physicians, the mainstream media, and teachers' union members, *all* insisting that masks must be worn to protect others. Conservative Republicans, concerned that mandating mask-wearing was an unacceptable impingement on their First Amendment rights were criticized as being "anti-science" or worse.

It is likely that many will continue to wear their masks until someone in authority of their favored political stripe insists that they stop, and possibly even after that. As it stands now, no one in authority appears to be inclined to take an anxious public's "security blanket" away. If the truth were told, many would have to admit that they had been wrong all along, and that's something that they are not inclined to do.

SOCIAL DISTANCING

Viral spread falls off inversely with distance, so social distancing was understandably seen as a possibly effective strategy for diminishing viral transmission. In the past, this would have been achieved by quarantining those with signs of illness. It has not previously been used as a strategy to separate those who are well from each other. It is true that asymptomatic individuals can be infected, but generalized social distancing has never been a public health strategy in the past, except when there was a possibility of containing a virus early in its initial spread. Nor has an entire population even been defined as "infected" based on highly sensitive PCR results. The truth is that despite being a rational approach, there is no convincing evidence that social distancing was effective in stopping the spread of COVID-19. (Berenson, 2020)

Whereas the widely adopted mandatory six-feet of separation was initially thought to be protective, that guideline was never tested. Instead, it was arbitrarily chosen based on nineteenth-century studies designed to prevent the spread of tuberculosis, a disease caused by a much less infectious mycobacterial species. As a result of this ill-conceived suggestion, indoor and outdoor spaces were painted with circles six feet apart. Subsequent studies showed that distances as small as three feet were sufficient to reduce the transmission of coronavirus spread.

As previously noted, the greatest risk of viral spread occurs indoors in poorly ventilated areas, and when in proximity to someone who is symptomatically infected. Once again, what might sound like a sound policy failed when tested.

POPULATION LOCKDOWNS

One of the conclusions that have emerged from the pandemic is that population lockdowns have been ineffective at limiting infection COVID-19, but do have dire negative consequences with respect to other health issues, child education, and the economy. Indeed, there is good evidence that the rate of infections has actually been worse when lockdowns were imposed. (Berenson, 2020) The reasons are worthy of further consideration. First, lockdowns increase the time spent indoors, where ventilation is often poor. When families are forced to live indoors with a family member who is infected, there is a high likelihood that everyone in the household will contract the virus.

The emergence of mutated strains of coronavirus with increased infectivity may inadvertently be fostered by lockdowns, as mutations emerge due to pressure on the virus to identify viable hosts. This is reduced with lockdowns and potentially could foster the selection of new mutated strains.

The initial idea of imposing lockdowns to "flatten the curve" of infection, when there was a potential danger of overwhelming health-care facilities was reasonable. But prolonged lockdowns have been of no benefit and should have been discontinued and *never* reinstated once this was recognized. Lockdowns have benefitted no one except online vendors, like *Amazon*, and large businesses that were excluded from the lockdowns for inexplicable reasons, along with political officials, who took them as an opportunity to expand executive powers. States that chose not to impose lockdowns, or to close schools, have fared better than, or at least as well as, states that imposed prolonged lockdowns, not only economically as might be expected but also with respect to mortality from COVID-19. Unfortunately, lockdowns are still being imposed on an increasingly unhappy public in areas of Europe and Australia and are poised to re-emerge as a strategy in the US.

THERAPIES FOR COVID-19

Assessing therapeutic efficacy is a far more complicated issue than is generally appreciated. One factor that routinely confounds determining therapeutic efficacy is the *placebo response* (R. Kradin, 2008). Most physicians do not have a proper understanding of what *placebo effects* are, as they are rarely considered in medical school, likely because they represent an area of near "mystical" ineffability. But what can be said about them is that they are not fictitious responses seen only in anxious suggestible women, as used to be a common explanation. Instead, virtually *all* therapies show placebo effects, including those that are judged as effective independent of subjective factors. In other words, even drugs like antibiotics can show placebo effects in clinical trials.

One of the factors that appear to evoke placebo responses is a patient's assessment of the competence of his physician. The therapeutic relationship is an *asymmetric* one, with physicians perceived as having healing "powers" that patients do not. Placebo responses were likely responsible for the positive effects of most pre-modern therapeutics, which is why their continued presence is a source of embarrassment for medical scientists.

The prevailing Progressive emphasis on *equity* seeks to deny asymmetric interpersonal power dynamics and instead attempts to convey the notion that there is no meaningful distinction between doctor and patient, and that being an informed patient somehow improves therapeutic outcomes by diminishing such power-based distinctions. But there is no evidence to support the claim that therapeutic responses are improved by leveling the playing field between doctor and patient.

Years ago, my research team developed a novel immunological experimental therapy trial for the treatment of cancer (R. Kradin et al., 1989). It received widespread media attention, and I was flooded with requests for the treatment. The regimen required several weeks in hospital and had uncomfortable side effects. Most of those enrolled in the trial had researched the protocol in hope of a cure. They read the medical literature, asked probing questions, and at times offered suggestions as to how the treatment might be improved.

One of the subjects was a retired construction worker whose daughter was a nurse who had read about the treatment and requested that he receive it. The man knew little about his disease or the treatment, other than what his daughter had told him. He asked few questions, and at one point turned to me and said, "Doc, do whatever you think is best. I trust you."

About 20 percent of patients in the trial achieved partial anti-tumor responses, i.e., greater than a 25 percent reduction in the bulk of their tumors, but this man had a complete response with no detectable residual cancer. Although he would eventually die from a recurrence of his cancer, he had a prolonged period of being tumor-free.

The story is an anecdote, and it would be wrong to draw any general conclusions from it. Whether this man's faith played a role in his response, I cannot say. Faith is something that Progressives, scientists, and most physicians, put little stock in. Invested in what they imagine to be rational, they tend to dismiss faith as superstition. However, it is an integral part of the human psychological repertoire, and as such should not be ignored. As Shakespeare notes in *Hamlet,* "There are more things in heaven and Earth, Horatio, than are dreamt of in your philosophy [science]." Understandably, doctors should base their medical practice on science, but those who denigrate other aspects of mind/body activity may unwittingly be undermining the success of their treatments.

Fewer today are willing to place their fate in the hands of another than in the past. As a society, we are losing this ability and may be suffering as a result. Physicians are not inclined to accept that their "power" as healers could possibly extend to factors beyond their medical knowledge and expertise. When I have tried to explain placebo responses to young physicians, they invariably react with disbelief. As a result of their education, they eschew the notion that healing can be achieved, in part, through psychological factors, despite a mountain of evidence to support that conclusion. (R. L. Kradin, 2004)

Before considering the specific therapeutic measures available for COVID-19, it must be emphasized again that the risk of dying from the virus is low even for the elderly. More than 700,000 deaths in the US have currently been attributed to "COVID-19," but it is not possible to determine whether this number accurately reflects deaths caused *by* COVID-19. An uncertain but possibly large number of so-called "COVID-19 deaths" have been documented in people who died from other causes that were either certified as having had or were thought to have had concomitant evidence of COVID-19 infection (Berenson, 2020). In a recent televised interview, Dr. Walensky admitted that ~75 percent of those dying with COVID-19 had at least four major risk factors and would likely have died independently of COVID-19 infection. There have been cases of deaths due to gunshot wounds recorded as "COVID-related deaths." The reasons have to do with financial incentives to hospitals for recording deaths as "COVID-related":

> Medicare will pay hospitals a 20 percent "add-on" to the regular payment for COVID-19 patients. That's a result of the CARES Act, the largest of the three federal stimulus laws enacted in response to the coronavirus, which was signed into law March 27. ("Hospitals get paid more to list patients as COVID-19," 2020)

REMDESIVIR

A new antiviral drug, Remdesivir, was initially demonstrated to have beneficial effects in clinical trials in patients with COVID-19. In November of 2020, the results of a multicentered NIAID study showed that Remdesivir was superior to placebos in shortening the time to recovery in adults hospitalized with COVID-19 and evidence of lower respiratory tract infection. (Beigel, Tomashek, Dodd, & al, 2020)

The drug had initially been developed by Gilead Sciences for other purposes, and Dr. Fauci pushed hard for its approval by the FDA. Microsoft's founder Bill Gates, who has worked closely with Fauci in the past on HIV-AIDS, owns a substantial number of shares in Gilead Sciences (Kennedy Jr., 2021).

But following its approval, subsequent experience with the drug raised substantial concerns about its efficacy as well as the FDA approval process. According to an article in the prestigious journal *Science*:

> October was a good month for Gilead Sciences, the giant manufacturer of antivirals headquartered in Foster City, California. On 8 October, the company inked an agreement to supply the European Union with its drug Remdesivir as a treatment for COVID-19—a deal potentially worth more than $1 billion. Two weeks later, on October 22, the US Food and Drug Administration (FDA) approved Remdesivir for use against the pandemic coronavirus SARS-CoV-2 in the United States—the first drug to receive that status. The EU and US decisions pave the way for Gilead's drug into two major markets, both with soaring COVID-19 cases.

> But both decisions baffled scientists who have closely watched the clinical trials of Remdesivir unfold over the past six months—and who have many questions about Remdesivir's worth. At best, one large, well-designed study found Remdesivir modestly reduced the time to recover from COVID-19 in hospitalized patients with severe illness. A few smaller studies found no impact of treatment on the disease whatsoever. Then, on October 15—in this month's decidedly unfavorable news for Gilead—the fourth and largest controlled study delivered what some believed was a coup de grâce: The World Health Organization's (WHO's) Solidarity trial showed that Remdesivir does not reduce mortality or the time COVID-19 patients take to recover.

> *Science* has learned that both FDA's decision and the EU deal came about under unusual circumstances that gave the company important advantages. FDA never consulted a group of outside experts that it has at the ready to weigh in on complicated antiviral drug issues. That group, the Antimicrobial Drugs Advisory Committee (AMDAC), mixes infectious disease clinicians with biostatisticians, pharmacists, and a consumer representative to review all available data on experimental treatments and make recommendations to FDA about drug approvals—yet it has not convened once during the pandemic.

> The European Union, meanwhile, decided to settle on the Remdesivir pricing exactly one week before the disappointing Solidarity trial

results came out. It was unaware of those results, although Gilead, having donated Remdesivir to the trial, was informed of the data on September 23 and knew the trial was a bust.

"This is a very, very bad look for the FDA, and the dealings between Gilead and EU make it another layer of badness," says Eric Topol, a cardiologist at the Scripps Research Translational Institute who objected to Remdesivir's FDA approval. (Cohen & Kupferschmidt, 2020)

In a setting in which people are desperate to find effective treatments, it is troubling that Dr. Fauci and *Big Pharma* would have pressured the FDA to approve an ineffective drug. But this is only one of many potential conflicts that surround Fauci and *Big Pharma*.

Hydroxychloroquine

Arguably the most publicized controversy surrounding COVID-19 treatments involves the use of hydroxychloroquine (HCQ). The drug has been used for decades in the treatment and prophylaxis of malaria, and millions have used it safely. It has been effective for this purpose and it carries minimal risk when taken at the prescribed dosage.[33] In addition to its anti-malarial effects, HCQ is used for the treatment of autoimmune disorders, such as lupus erythematosus, because of its potent anti-inflammatory effects.

Early in the pandemic, reports from China and from the renowned French infectious disease specialist Didier Raoult suggested early use of HCQ, with or without concomitant administration of the antibiotic azithromycin, reduced symptoms and mortality from COVID-19

---

[33] Many portions of the world where malaria is endemic are currently resistant to chloroquine.

(Gautret, J, P., & al, 2020). [34] But unlike Remdesivir, HCQ is no longer patent-protected and can be purchased for just a few dollars on the open market.

As the pandemic unfolded in March of 2020, President Trump announced during one of his televised COVID-19 conferences that the FDA would fast-track approval of unproven coronavirus treatments, including chloroquine and HCQ. Said Trump, "The nice part is, it's been around for a long time, so we know that if things don't go as planned, it's not going to kill anybody."

The response to Trump's announcement was immediate and unprecedented. Dr. Fauci took the opportunity to publicly announce that the success of HCQ was "anecdotal," and should be ignored until a detailed randomized placebo-controlled trial could be conducted. He further suggested that the drug could be "dangerous" for those with COVID-19, with no evidence to support that claim (Kennedy Jr., 2021). Curiously, this high standard of scientific proof was something that Fauci had not insisted upon for any of his other recommendations to the public, including masks, lockdowns, social distancing, and Remdesivir.

The mainstream media, always trawling for new opportunities to discredit Trump, amplified Fauci's warnings. In one well-publicized case of a man who had mistakenly identified an additive to an aquarium cleaner for chloroquine and died following its ingestion, the media blamed Trump for the death.

As previously noted, the *Lancet*, a once widely respected medi-

---

34 Raoult was one of eleven prominent scientists named to a committee to advise on scientific matters pertaining to the epidemic in France. He did not attend any of the meetings and resigned from the committee, saying that he refused to participate. He denounced the "absence of anything scientifically sound," and criticized its members for "not having a clue." He defended chloroquine, saying that it had suddenly been declared dangerous after having been safely used for eighty years. Following reports and a complaint filed in July by the French-speaking Society of Infectious Pathology, the departmental council of the French Order of Physicians opened a formal case against Didier Raoult.

cal journal, published a study that appeared to discredit the efficacy of HCQ and supported the notion that it was potentially toxic. But careful readers noted problems with the study and brought them to the editors' attention. Subsequently, the study was retracted, as the data could not be produced and there was an uncomfortable implication that it may have been fabricated.

But by then, the reputation of the HCQ had been irreparably damaged. Despite the fact that many physicians had used it through the pandemic with apparent success, Fauci and the media continued to insist that it was ineffective, and upped the ante by suggesting that anyone who touted its success was spreading "misinformation." The social media giants, *Facebook*, and *Twitter*, moved in quickly to "cancel" anyone, including expert physicians and scientists who suggested that HCQ might be an effective treatment for COVID-19. When a large study indicated that it was ineffective in patients with *advanced* disease, which no one had previously disputed, Fauci took the opportunity to put a final nail in the drug's coffin.

In an unprecedented move, the FDA then revoked the emergency use of the drug, in a June 2020 letter (Hinton, 2020):

The agency determined that the legal criteria for issuing an EUA are no longer met. Based on its ongoing analysis of the EUA and emerging scientific data, the FDA determined that chloroquine and hydroxychloroquine are unlikely to be effective in treating COVID-19 for the authorized uses in the EUA. Additionally, in light of ongoing serious cardiac adverse events and other potential serious side effects, the known and potential benefits of chloroquine and hydroxychloroquine no longer outweigh the known and potential risks for the authorized use. This is the statutory standard for issuance of an EUA. The Biomedical Advanced Research and Development Authority (BARDA) within the US Department of Health and Human Services originally requested the EUA covering chloroquine and hydroxychloroquine, and the FDA granted the

EUA on March 28, 2020, based on the science and data available at the time. Today, in consultation with the FDA, BARDA sent a letter to the FDA requesting revocation of the EUA based on up-to-date science and data.

"We've made clear throughout the public health emergency that our actions will be guided by science and that our decisions may evolve as we learn more about the SARS-CoV-2 virus, review the latest data, and consider the balance of risks versus benefits of treatments for COVID-19," said FDA Deputy Commissioner for Medical and Scientific Affairs Anand Shah, MD. "The FDA always underpins its decision-making with the most trustworthy, high-quality, up-to-date evidence available. We will continue to examine all of the emergency use authorizations the FDA has issued and make changes, as appropriate, based on emerging evidence."

All the while, studies continued to appear demonstrating HCQ's apparent efficacy against COVID-19. But now some states and large chain pharmacies refused to honor prescriptions written by physicians for HCQ:

Many states have restricted pharmacists from dispensing certain medications unless it is specifically being prescribed for FDA-approved use. Additionally, the American Medical Association, American Pharmacists Association, and American Society of Health-System Pharmacists issued a joint statement discouraging doctors and pharmacists from inappropriately prescribing medications such as hydroxychloroquine and chloroquine. This is to help prevent medication stockpiling and potential drug shortages. (AMA, 2020)

It is important to understand the implications of this ban and how unusual a step this was. Virtually all new medications go through an FDA-approval process that establishes safety and efficacy in randomized placebo-controlled trials. But once a drug has been approved, physicians are free to use it for "off-label" purposes, if they have reason to believe that it may have beneficial effects. Considering the limited treatment options for COVID-19, the fact that many physicians continued to claim benefits from their experience with the drug and the minimal side-effect profile associated with its use, it would be standard operating procedure for a physician and patient to decide together whether to try using HCQ "off-label." I know of no other instance when the AMA and pharmacists have conspired to block physicians' access to a previously approved drug. This is an example of the top-down government influence that has been imposed on the medical profession and society-at-large during the current pandemic.

It would be naïve to ignore the possibility that factors other than medical science figured into the HCQ ban. Considering that a treatment course of Remdesivir costs ~$3,200, i.e., four hundred times as much as treatment with HCQ (~$8 per course), the financial incentive to discourage the widespread use of HCQ is clear. Historically, Fauci has had close ties with *Big Pharma* over the years, so it is not surprising that he would bolster claims for an expensive drug like Remdesivir while denigrating the possible efficacy of an off-label cheap one. That might be excusable if Remdesivir were genuinely effective, which does not appear to be the case. Companies collaborating with research being performed at the NIH as well as the Gates Foundation, include Bayer, BD, bioMérieux, Boehringer Ingelheim, Bristol-Myers Squibb, Eisai, Eli Lilly, GSK, Johnson & Johnson, Merck, Novartis, Pfizer, Sanofi, and *Gilead*—certainly not a short list. (Kennedy Jr., 2021)

Finally, it is worth noting how the term "misinformation" has been used for political purposes to silence dissent. If information that was critical of the government's public health response were untrue, it would have been labeled as such. But it has not, because "misinformation" does not mean that the information is false; rather, it is a totalitarian strategy of "doublespeak" that equates to *any* information that does not support the government's official position. Indeed, the bulk of the "misinformation" surrounding the pandemic has come from the government and mainstream media, not from other sources. Criticisms of lockdowns, mask mandates, vaccine mandates, etc., were all labeled "misinformation," but have ultimately been demonstrated to have been correct.

IVERMECTIN

The response to ivermectin resembles that described for HCQ. Ivermectin is an FDA-approved drug primarily used to treat certain parasitic worms, head lice, and skin conditions like rosacea. But it has shown potent antiviral properties in test-tube experiments. When reports surfaced that it might be effective in treating early COVID-19 infection, the CDC quickly warned against its use, and Dr. Fauci, in his now predictable manner, did everything possible to discourage its use. In a statement, he argued that:

> "I want to be really clear. There is no data supporting that ivermectin prevents or cures COVID-19," he said. "Unfortunately, the promotion for this drug has spread like wildfire among conspiracy theorists and people who are out to make a profit, and we're seeing people buy it from vets and take it themselves with really serious consequences. Another example of the very real harm of misinformation. (Taliesen, 2021)

Note not only the claim that the drug does not work but also the fear-mongering statement that patients might take veterinary dosages and die. This is Fauci's usual MO.

Yet, a recent meta-analysis conducted by Bryant and researchers at NIH contradicts Fauci's conclusion. According to these researchers:

> Meta-analysis of 15 trials found that ivermectin reduced risk of death compared with no ivermectin (average risk ratio 0.38, 95 percent confidence interval 0.19–0.73; n = 2438; I2 = 49 percent; moderate-certainty evidence). This result was confirmed in a trial

sequential analysis using the same DerSimonian–Laird method that underpinned the unadjusted analysis. This was also robust against a trial sequential analysis using the Biggerstaff–Tweedie method. Low-certainty evidence found that ivermectin prophylaxis reduced COVID-19 infection by an average 86 percent (95 percent confidence interval 79 percent–91 percent). Secondary outcomes provided less certain evidence. Low-certainty evidence suggested that there may be no benefit with ivermectin for "need for mechanical ventilation," whereas effect estimates for "improvement" and "deterioration" clearly favored ivermectin use. Severe adverse events were rare among treatment trials and evidence of no difference was assessed as low certainty. Evidence on other secondary outcomes was very low certainty. Moderate-certainty evidence finds that large reductions in COVID-19 deaths are possible using ivermectin. Using ivermectin early in the clinical course may reduce numbers progressing to severe disease. The apparent safety and low cost suggest that ivermectin is likely to have a significant impact on the SARS-CoV-2 pandemic globally. (Bryant, Lawrie, & Dowswell, 2021)

Several independent studies have duplicated these findings and have concluded that ivermectin is both safe and effective in the early treatment of COVID-19. Nevertheless, one hears nothing about these studies from Fauci, the CDC, the Biden administration, or the media. The cost of ivermectin? About $100 per treatment course. Another potentially interesting finding is that countries where HCQ and ivermectin are used regularly for treatment of malaria and parasitic infection have reported less mortality from COVID-19 compared to the US and other Western countries. (Kennedy Jr., 2021)

When the popular podcast hoist Joe Rogan announced that he had been treated successfully for COVID-19 with ivermectin, the media took the opportunity to pounce and discredit him, as an article from the *Rolling Stone* magazine suggests:

But most media reports of Rogan's COVID-19 diagnosis focused on the fact that he had said he had also taken ivermectin. An antiparasitic drug, ivermectin is perhaps best known as a deworming medication for horses or dogs (though it is indeed prescribed to humans in tablet form to treat parasitic infection, or in topical form to treat conditions like rosacea). As *Rolling Stone* has previously reported, in recent months ivermectin has been promoted heavily by right-wing media personalities like Laura Ingraham as a potential treatment for COVID-19, despite the fact that there is little consistent evidence to support its use in this regard; as a result, people have been buying the drug in bulk, raving about its efficacy in private Facebook groups and griping about its side effects after taking too high a dose (which include uncontrollable defecation). The FDA has warned against taking ivermectin as a treatment for COVID, saying that overdoses could lead to side effects such as dizziness, seizures, and increased vomiting; and some states have reported that people taking overdoses of ivermectin has led to an increase in poison control calls. (Dickson, 2021)

Indeed, until December of 2021, the only off-label drugs approved for use in the treatment of COVID-19 were corticosteroids, which are used so widely that it would be virtually impossible to deny them to physicians without evoking a backlash. The theme that has emerged from the experience with therapeutics in the pandemic has been that expensive new drugs that are still "on label" for *Big Pharma* have been greeted enthusiastically by Dr. Fauci and the CDC, whereas cheap off-label drugs have been denigrated and banned. This means that many patients have been denied access to potentially life-saving medications possibly in order to line the coffers of *Big Pharma*. We do not know how many lives may have been lost as a result, but the number could be large.

MONOCLONAL ANTIBODIES

Regeneron is the trade name of a cocktail of humanized neutralizing monoclonal antibodies that react with a limited number of coronavirus antigens. Regen-Cov received an emergency use authorization (EUA) from the Food and Drug Administration in November 2020 for the treatment of high-risk outpatients with mild-to-moderate COVID-19.

Regen-Cov is included in the NIH treatment guidelines for high-risk outpatients with COVID-19. The data from a phase-three trial involving outpatients with COVID-19 showed that Regen-Cov reduced the risk of COVID-19–related hospitalization or death and sped up the time to recovery. This treatment achieved a degree of notoriety when it was publicized that President Trump received both Regeneron and Remdesivir when he contracted COVID-19 in the Fall of 2020, weeks prior to the presidential election. Critics argued that since the drug was not yet widely available that it was "inequitable" for the President to have received special treatment, a notion that flies in the face of common sense, considering that Trump, at the time, was the President of the United States, and leader of the Free World. But making sense is not a Progressive strongpoint.[35]

In January of 2022, the FDA withdrew Regeneron from the market, claiming that it was not effective at neutralizing the omicron variant. However, the official recommendation was that the public continue to receive "boosters" with vaccines that have been proven ineffective at reducing the incidence of disease or its spread and that react with comparable antigenic epitopes as the vaccines.

MOLNUPIRAVIR

In November of 2021, a panel of experts advising the Food and Drug Administration voted in favor of emergency use authorization of Molnupiravir, an antiviral pill from Merck and Ridgeback Biotherapeutics, to treat COVID-19.

---

35 The state of Florida had set up clinics statewide where Regeneron was made available to those with COVID-19 who were judged to be at high risk for morbidity and death. Recently, the Biden administration, which controls the distribution of the antibodies reduced the amount given to Florida, while in the midst of political squabbles with the Governor DeSantis, who has argued against vaccine mandates and lockdowns in his state.

Molnupiravir is an oral antiviral treatment for COVID-19 that can be taken orally at home. A second oral drug from Pfizer, Paxlovid, received FDA approval in December 2021 (Griffin, 2021). Both drugs are intended for use by people with mild to moderate illness, at high risk of developing severe COVID-19, and should be taken within five days of symptoms. An interim analysis of a clinical study of the drug found that Molnupiravir reduced the risk of hospitalization or death in half. Among people who got the drug, 7 percent ended up in the hospital or died, compared with 14 percent who received a placebo. However, an FDA summary showed that in the second half of the study, patients in the group treated with the drug were more likely to have been hospitalized or die than those who received placebo, which means that the protective effects against death seen in the first half of the study were no longer present in the second half. When asked about this discrepancy, Dr. Nicholas Kartsonis, a Merck senior vice president, simply replied that, "I don't have a satisfying answer to your question." That's a fair answer but should cast doubt on the efficacy of the drug.

Molnupiravir inhibits viral propagation by introducing errors in the viral genome. The biochemical and structural basis of how it induces lethal mutagenesis has largely been unexplored. However, the possibility that it may drive the emergence of new mutant strains of COVID-19 that are unresponsive to vaccines or therapeutics is a concern.

The possibility of birth defects was also raised by the panel of reviewers at the FDA, leading to reservations about prescribing the drug to pregnant people. "I don't think you can ethically say it's okay to give this drug in pregnancy, obviously," said Dr. Janet Cragan of the Centers for Disease Control and Prevention. "But at the same time, I'm not sure you can ethically tell a pregnant woman who has COVID-19 that she can't have the drug if she's decided that's what she needs." (Hensley, 2021)

The data indicate that the efficacy and safety of this new drug are at best questionable. In the past, it would likely not have received FDA approval. Nor has it been made widely available to the public. In the setting of coronavirus hysteria and pressures from *Big Pharma* and the Biden administration, the usual rules do not apply. And nowhere has this been more obvious than in the development of vaccines.

VACCINES

Vaccination is a standard approach to reducing the risk of infection in a large population. The first vaccine originally termed "inoculation" was introduced by William Jenner in 1798 as protection against small-pox. Today, vaccines are routinely administered for a host of bacterial and viral infections. It was clear that a vaccine ideally would be the best *protective* regimen against SARS-CoV2, and experience suggested that after sufficient numbers of people had either recovered from the virus or been vaccinated that "herd immunity" would emerge, which means that the probability of interpersonal spread would be markedly reduced.

The number of individuals that need to have some degree of immunity for "herd immunity" to occur is unknown, and guestimates have ranged from 70 to 90 percent. However, when lockdowns are adopted as the primary response to an infection, the possibility of achieving herd immunity, in the absence of a mass vaccination strategy is reduced, and this was an argument against imposing lockdowns. Many of the deaths due to COVID-19 could have almost certainly been avoided, if high-risk populations had been targeted for quarantine, rather than locking down the entire population for whom the risk of severe disease was low. Questions to health officials as to when host immunity has been achieved and whether it will then be safe to return to normal life, have never been adequately answered, and mass vaccination makes little sense if it does not lead to the normalization of daily life.

Dr. Fauci has placed an extraordinary emphasis on the development of a vaccine for COVID-19, as he did for HIV-1 (he was not successful), and there has been a general lack of enthusiasm shown by the NIH and CDC for non-vaccine therapeutics. While it is true that most anti-viral therapies are only marginally effective, the same can be said about the efficacy of most vaccines directed at rapidly mutating respiratory viral pathogens.

If past experience is a guide, the likelihood of eradicating COVID-19 via a vaccine is almost nil. The commonsensical approach therefore would have been to make efforts to protect the most vulnerable in society, i.e., the elderly and those with underlying risk factors, while developing a vaccine that might prove less than fully effective and administering therapeutics when people were ill. Other than that, people should have been encouraged to go on with their lives as before the pandemic, with the understanding that although some were bound to contract the infection, more than 99 percent would survive. You don't have to be a Las Vegas bookmaker to recognize those are pretty good odds. But this is not the messaging that has been coming from our health experts, politicians, or the media, for the last two years.

"Leaky" Vaccines

An ideal vaccine confers protection against infection. It also has long-lasting protective effects. When a child is vaccinated for measles or polio, they develop lifelong protection from infection. Indeed, vaccines against a variety of non-respiratory pathogens that do not mutate confer lifetime protection.

An individual's ability to transmit infection should also be abrogated by an effective vaccine. But the current data suggests that this is not the case for the current vaccines against COVID-19. Following what may have been an initial decrease in the incidence of new infections following vaccination, a new wave of infection was observed amongst the vaccinated. This may reflect new mutations that have made the vaccines less effective, as they are all directed against a limited number of antigenic epitopes in the "spike protein" of COVID-19, which is highly susceptible to mutations. So, vaccines can be expected to confer limited protection with time, and that's what has been observed.

Since fully vaccinated individuals can become ill and transmit the virus to others, the rational solution to this would be to either 1) rely primarily on therapeutics to save lives, 2) create new vaccines directed against virulent mutants, or 3) quarantine the high-risk population and allow the rest of society to develop natural immunity. None of these approaches has been suggested or implemented by our health experts, although efforts are apparently ongoing to create a vaccine against the omicron variant of COVID-19, which is already beginning to disappear. Instead, there has been an irrational push to repetitively boost immunity with the original vaccines that are known to be ineffective. The rationale that antibody levels against the original antigenic epitopes are "boosted," is a finding of no clinical relevance.[36] The argument that the vaccine protects against severe disease and death has not been distinguished from the possibility that the omicron variant is simply less virulent, and therefore less likely to cause severe disease and death, as appears to be the case.

NOVEL VACCINE METHODOLOGY

The current approach to vaccination for COVID-19 is novel both in its methodology and the speed at which it was brought to market.

---

36 The rational for this approach has once again been flawed. The major justification has been that antibody levels against the spike protein are boosted by repetitive vaccinations. But this does not necessarily indicate a protective effect. Rather, it means that the immune system is capable of responding to the original antigen. But once the virus has mutated, that finding has no relevance!

It is based on two distinct molecular strategies. One is the injection of a selected coronavirus mRNA sequence that encodes for the native COVID-19 spike (S) protein. Following injection, the viral mRNA is translated by the recipient's cells into viral spike proteins that are expressed and can elicit a host immune response. The other involves injecting a sample of a corresponding viral DNA sequence, which is then translated into viral spike protein antigens to elicit an immune response.

As originally conceived, the mRNA vaccines required two separate injections spaced 2–3 weeks apart, whereas the DNA vaccine required only one. This was determined by small phase-one studies that examined the levels of antibody elicited by these injections. Phase-three clinical testing suggested that the mRNA vaccines might provide greater protection, with greater than 90 percent protection reported in the mRNA-treated subjects versus ~70 percent protection from the one-time DNA vaccine. The initial side effect profile for both approaches was reported as minimal, but untoward side effects and rare deaths have been observed. As to the potential long-term side effects, i.e., potential adverse reactions occurring months, years, or decades after vaccination, the answer is that is currently anybody's guess. (Kennedy Jr., 2021)[37]

One of the potential pitfalls in clinical medicine is imagining that "rational" explanations necessarily suffice for predicting actual clinical responses, as there are numerous examples of well-reasoned therapeutic approaches that have failed in practice. (R. Kradin, 2008). We are only beginning to have some sense of the long-term efficacy of mass vaccinations based on data from other countries, particularly Israel, where greater than 90 percent of the population has received at least

---

37 There has been a concerted effort to avoid monitoring side effects following the vaccine. It is almost impossible to get accurate data on this topic. And as is usually the case, the vaccine developers are given legal immunity from tort litigation.

two doses of an mRNA vaccine. Initially, the vaccination appeared to be protective, but that impression was undermined by the emergence of new variants capable of causing infection. Following an initial decline following vaccination, new cases began to appear in fully vaccinated individuals (Berenson, 2020). Furthermore, it became apparent that vaccinated persons were capable of spreading the disease. The experience in the US has been similar.

The argument made by President Biden and Dr. Fauci that new cases represented a "pandemic of the unvaccinated" is false. Instead, both unvaccinated and vaccinated individuals have contracted infection. Whereas mortality *may* be reduced amongst those who have been vaccinated, it is not clear that decreased deaths can be attributed to the vaccine or to changes in the virus that have made it less virulent. It is unseemly for politicians to make arguments to escape blame for not being able to control the pandemic as promised, but it is unquestionably unethical for Fauci and others in the medical profession to make such claims, as they know better.

Why has the vaccination program failed to protect greater than 90 percent of the population as initially promised? There are multiple possible explanations. One is that older patients, i.e., those most susceptible to serious infection can fail to mount a protective antibody response to vaccines due to the effects of age on the immune system.[38] One out of three elderly individuals fails to mount a vigorous antibody response to vaccines (Berenson, 2020). There is no convincing evidence that "boosters" benefit these individuals.

Another reason is that when *Big Pharma* selects subjects for its clinical trials, it purposefully excludes the elderly. This improves the vaccine's probability of success. Scrutiny of the data from the initial

---

38 The immune system tends to fail with age. The elderly may not be able to stimulate protective antibody protection, either as well as younger individuals, or at all in some cases.

Pfizer study that led to the approval of its vaccine showed that the initial 95 percent reduction in death was accounted for by a total of *two* deaths in the vaccinated group of greater than 13,000, versus *one* in the placebo arm of the study, hardly a hearty difference. But this is how data can be manipulated and interpreted to reach hyperbolic conclusions. Indeed, when deaths from all causes were reviewed at the end of the Pfizer vaccine trial, more deaths were seen in the *vaccinated* group, raising the possibility of vaccine-related (antibody-enhanced) mortality.

If history is a guide, researchers should have suspected that 95 percent protection for a vaccine directed against a respiratory virus was an unprecedented result. The average influenza vaccine confers less than 50 percent protection each year. Even though the coronavirus vaccine strategies are novel, public health experts should have cautioned the public that this level of protection was likely exaggerated. But in their rush to reassure an anxious public, make money for *Big Pharma,* and claim political success, they chose not to. Now the nation's health leaders and politicians are so entangled in falsehoods and exaggerations that they are at a loss as to how best to "spin" the narrative to a disgruntled public.

And the rush to commercialize a new finding has not been limited to vaccines and drugs during the pandemic. Indeed, it has become the rule, especially in the area of testing, that new test kits may be immediately offered to the public even before they have been adequately standardized and shown to be accurate if third-party payers can be convinced to cover the costs. If there is money to be made, all stops will be pulled out by biotech firms and the corporate hospital to proceed.

The issue of vaccine-related morbidity and mortality, which understandably concerns many who refuse to be vaccinated, has been consistently ignored by regulators, public health officials, and the media. Reported cases of complications have been many-fold higher following these new vaccines than were historically observed in the older vaccine strategy trials (Kennedy Jr., 2021). There have been cases and deaths from autoimmune thrombocytopenia (decrease in blood-clotting elements), Guillain-Barre syndrome (an ascending paralysis), a slew of cases of myocarditis (heart inflammation), which is a serious and potentially deadly disorder, mostly in young healthy males who are not at high risk for serious disease from COVID-19. The recent study that shows that those who have had COVID-19 may be at markedly increased risk of heart disease is disturbing, and it is currently unknown whether having been vaccinated may also confer an increased risk for cardiovascular disease. (Sidik, 2022)[39]

Respiratory viruses, including coronaviruses, tend to mutate, especially in vaccinated populations, as vaccination increases mutation pressure for the virus.[40] A series of mutations have occurred in COVID-19 but only the delta variant has been associated with considerable morbidity.[41] Initial reports of a new strain of a heavily mutated virus from South Africa, the omicron variant, have to date not been associated with considerable morbidity.

The duration of immunity following vaccination is uncertain. Estimates of sixty days to six months are based on guesswork and should not be used to inform vaccination strategies. Furthermore, testing for circulating anti-COVID-19 antibodies may not be a good approach on which to base a population-based strategy, as antibody levels can fall to undetectable levels but then increase rapidly when the host encoun-

---

39 This is a real concern as many cardiac pathologies, e.g., rheumatic fever and cardiac valvular disease, are mediated by aberrant immune responses to pathogens rather than by direct cardiac damage attributable to infection.

40 The reason is simple and has to do with Darwinian competition. When the population becomes increasingly immune to a virus, mutants have an advantage with respect to their spread.

41 The mutant variants are labeled by convention with the Greek alphabet from *alpha* to *omega*. In what may be the most absurd expression of political correctness the Greek letter *xi* was purposefully skipped so as not to offend the Chinese leader Xi-Jinping.

ters the virus again due to immune memory (anamnestic response) and because they do not assess cell-mediated immunity. Repeat infections, should they occur, may prove to be attenuated compared to those seen in an immunologically naïve host.

Currently, we do not know with certainty how effective vaccination-induced humoral immunity will be over the long term. Nevertheless, it is not feasible to mass-vaccinate populations every few months. When new variants emerge, which they almost surely will, reflex plans to impose new restrictions, mask mandates, lockdowns, and repetitive vaccinations, make little sense, and will only lead to further health and economic disruptions without controlling the infection. Physicians who do not recognize this are responding to fictional narratives rather than to science or common sense.

As opposed to the single injection of a heat-killed virus, which was the standard for vaccines in the past, these genetically-driven approaches potentially allow the target protein-antigens they generate to be over-expressed on the surfaces of cells. This can potentially foster auto-immune reactions to normal tissues, including blood vessels, leading to endothelial injury, *in situ* thrombosis, and the entrapment of platelets in clots, resulting in a syndrome characterized both by excessive clotting and bleeding following vaccination. For good reasons, it is highly debatable as to whether individuals should be repetitively vaccinated, especially with the same vaccine. Arguments that this improves the host response do not sufficiently take into consideration the potentially harmful effects of repeated vaccination. This reflects a poor understanding of how the immune system functions, as *more* is not necessarily *better*. Indeed, most reports of severe side effects to the vaccines have occurred at the time of repeat vaccination. Continuing to administer frequent "booster" vaccines is likely to add little to protective immunity but almost certainly will lead to more side effects.

ACQUIRED IMMUNITY AND VACCINES

There is no medical precedent for vaccinating individuals with normal immune systems who have previously recovered from a virus. Nor have Dr. Fauci or the CDC adequately explained why they are promoting repetitive vaccinations with vaccines that are ineffective against new variants. Furthermore, if new mutant strains of COVID-19 do not produce life-threatening disease in the previously vaccinated, there is *no* compelling reason to re-vaccinate an entire population. Of course, drug companies will benefit financially substantially from administering "boosters," paid for by taxpayers, and with no fear of liability should ill-effects ensue in the first few years.

A PANDEMIC OF FEAR

The ability of infectious diseases to incite fear is well recognized. In times of pandemic, a frightened public is prone to seek reasons for why a rapidly spreading disease cannot be contained. During the Black Death in the Middle Ages, marginalized groups within society were accused of being the cause of the plague and persecuted as a result. But we know today, that the Black Death was caused by a bacterium, not by witches, heretics, or Jews.

The current pandemic is caused by a virus, SARS-CoV2. Yet Dr. Fauci, the government, and mainstream media, and have gone to extraordinary lengths to scapegoat the unvaccinated for spreading disease. The primary accusation, which is that the pandemic has been spread by vaccine-denying Trump supporters, is fallacious. Furthermore, it ignores evidence that people of color, who Progressives count as members of their political base, are *least* likely to be vaccinated. According to CDC statistics:

As of November 30, 2021, CDC reported that race/ethnicity was known for 70 percent of people who had received at least one dose of the vaccine. Among this group, nearly six in ten were White (58 percent), 10 percent were Black, 19 percent were Hispanic, 6 percent were Asian, 1 percent were American Indian or Alaska Native (AIAN), and <1 percent were Native Hawaiian or Other Pacific Islander (NHOPI), while 6 percent reported multiple or another race. White people make up a smaller share of people who have received at least one dose (58 percent) and people who have recently received a vaccination (54 percent) compared to their share of the total population (61 percent). The same pattern is observed among Black people, who make up 10 percent of people who have received at least one dose and 10 percent of those recently vaccinated, compared to 12 percent of the population. In contrast, Hispanic people make up a larger share of vaccinated people (19 percent) and people who recently received a vaccination (21 percent) compared to their share of the total population (17 percent).... White people account for the largest share of people who remain unvaccinated. Black and Hispanic people have been less likely than their White counterparts to have received a vaccine over the course of the vaccination rollout, but these disparities have narrowed over time and largely closed for Hispanic people. (Ndugga , Hilll, Artiga, & Haldar, 2021)

The current administration cynically continues to scapegoat Trump supporters as "ignorant," and "selfish," and as lacking concern for their fellow man, as opposed to well-meaning citizens who 1) have had COVID-19 and see no rational reason to be vaccinated, 2) have genuine medical concerns and are understandably worried about unknown possible long-term effects of the new vaccines, 3) have religious objections to vaccines, 4) lack trust based on the frequent errors in health policy, and/or 5) do not believe that the government has the right to tell them what to do with their bodies. For the most part, their concerns have not been addressed in any intelligent way by government health experts. Instead, they have been dismissed as somehow invalid.

The argument that those who object to vaccine mandates are "anti-science" is not supported by facts. Many who oppose vaccine mandates have stated that they favor vaccinations and have been vaccinated, but they oppose government efforts at making them compulsory and resist imposing punitive measures on those who choose not to be vaccinated. Undermining the notion of a "pandemic of the unvaccinated" is the fact that substantial numbers of new cases of COVID-19 have occurred in individuals who have received two or three vaccinations, including the current Speaker of the House and the Vice President!

> Breakthrough COVID-19 cases happen in people who are fully vaccinated, and they seem to happen more frequently now that the delta variant is circulating widely and immunity may be waning among those who got the vaccine many months ago. All three available coronavirus vaccines are very good at protecting you against severe forms of COVID-19, but they are not 100 percent effective in preventing infection…. A study in Washington State gathered data from over four million fully vaccinated people. The data showed a rate of about 1 in 5,000 experienced a breakthrough infection between January 17 and August 21, 2021. More recently, some populations have shown breakthrough infection rates of approximately *one in one hundred* fully vaccinated people. (Maragakis & Kelen, 2021)

Despite all of this, the medical profession, in general, has supported these false claims.

Unfortunately, few making false accusations have been willing to admit that their facts and conclusions are incorrect. Instead, they continue to target unvaccinated conservatives, who they regard as the cause of all of America's woes. They are unwilling to admit that all measures to eradicate the virus have failed. As critics have noted:

> On November 9, Biden announced that he had created a task force to "limit the spread of the virus" on January 20, 2021, the date he will be sworn in. Throughout November, he continued to make statements on this topic: "I am not going to shut down the economy, period. I am going to shut down the virus," he stressed on November

19, rejecting the idea of a national lockdown. This stance is questionable. What means and tools does Biden—and, more widely, the American federal government—really have to fight COVID-19? (Genieys & Brown, 2020)

But why is the anxiety surrounding the pandemic so severe? In the present age of narcissism, as the social critic Christopher Lasch termed it, youth is given the highest priority, and thoughts of death are dismissed or considered "morbid" (Lasch, 1979). We are no longer accustomed to confronting death, and we live under the illusion that we can avoid it. Death today is sequestered in hospitals, and out of public view. In the age of antimicrobials, we imagine, incorrectly, that we are now safe from deadly infections.[42] But periodically, lethal pandemics challenge our narcissistic fantasies of invulnerability.

As noted, the best estimates of risk of death from coronavirus put them at less than 1 percent. Even the elderly are at low risk, with perhaps a ~1 percent risk of dying from coronavirus, unless they harbor multiple serious underlying conditions, in which case it may rise 8 percent. But this is not the public's perception. As Yale epidemiologist Harvey Risch has argued, what we are experiencing is not merely a global viral infection; rather, it is a "pandemic of fear" (Farris, 2021). Faced with the possibility of contracting a potentially deadly disease, what in the past would have been an understandable source of concern, has devolved into panic for many.

Are Americans more fearful than in the past? The answer appears to be yes. A recent Chapman Survey suggests that, "Companies routinely market unnecessary products that promise protection from imagined or exaggerated harms" (Bader, Baker, Day & Gordon, 2021). Americans

---

42 Resistance to antibiotics is a large problem in the treatment of bacterial infections. Many bacteria have become resistant, and new antibiotics that overcome resistance are becoming harder to identify. For example, penicillin that used to treat *pneumococcus*, the bacteria that causes most cases of pneumonia, is currently ineffective against the pathogen. Similar scenarios exist for a variety of common infections.

have grown "soft," unaccustomed to adversity and unwilling to make sacrifices. Indeed, in a world of moral relativism, the notion of sacrifice holds little appeal for many Americans.

In *Denial of Death*, the philosopher Ernst Becker noted that we all live in a state of denial when it comes to our own mortality (Becker, 1973). When the fear of death interrupts this universal ego defense, neuroticisms may ensue. The hypochondriac cannot effectively deny the *possibility* of death and suffers from a fixed and intrusive obsessional concern about it. Until recently, it would likely have been considered neurotic to withdraw from life in the face of a less than 1 percent risk of death. But neurotics are famously poor at accurately assessing risk, and they may oscillate between being overly cautious and excessively bold.

The current pandemic has been characterized by the inability of many to make a rational assessment of *actual* risk. So, what *are* the risks of succumbing to the coronavirus versus dying unexpectedly while driving a car? Or when we cross the street? Or when we travel on an airplane? Considering these examples will put the matter into perspective. `

Statistics indicate that there are approximately six million automobile accidents in the US each year. That corresponds to roughly 16,438 per day. 22,471 cause only property damage, but more than 37,000 Americans are expected to die in automobile crashes each year. According to the National Safety Council, the chance of dying from a motor vehicle crash is 1 in 103, i.e., roughly 1.0 percent, which is higher than the overall risk of dying from COVID-19 (estimated to be ~0.15 percent for non-aged healthy Americans).

How about crossing the street? In 2017, 5,977 pedestrians were killed in the United States. That's one death every eighty-eight minutes. Additionally, an estimated 137,000 pedestrians were treated in emergency departments for non-fatal injuries in 2017. This number is roughly on par with the risk of dying from COVID-19.

Based on these numbers, one might suggest that those who are concerned enough to socially distance during the pandemic might also consider not driving their cars or walking on the street. Perhaps the greatest problem with the public health response to COVID-19 has been its unwillingness to supply accurate and reassuring information concerning the actual risks associated with COVID-19. They have been guilty of fear-mongering and stoking anxieties amongst an already frightened public.

It is known that a larger percentage of individuals have been infected than have developed symptoms. The true mortality rate is considerably lower than the initially suggested 1–3 percent, and there are dramatic differences in mortality between the very young and the very old. To put these numbers into perspective with respect to the mortality seen each year with seasonal "flu," the risk of death from influenza is ~15 per 100,000 in a non-pandemic year or ~0.01 percent. That is less than for COVID-19 but not dramatically so. And the risks of a child dying from the "flu" exceed death from COVID-19. In 2020, only one death of a child less than five years of age was attributed to COVID-19, and a total of 172 children have died since the beginning of the pandemic, with virtually all having severe underlying conditions. In 2020, 188 children under five died from influenza, and most were apparently in good health. (Boyd, 2021)

America, once the "home of the free and the brave" has become a risk-averse society. Public health officials, ostensibly trained to assess the objective risk of illness, have—due to their own neuroticisms and ignorance—adopted the unattainable position that *any* risk of contracting COVID-19 is too great. They can't ensure the public's safety, but they continue to avoid telling that truth. When Joe Biden recently backtracked on his original claims to "stop the virus" and suggested that the federal government had no effective solution for the pandemic, his remark was greeted with scorn from both sides of the culture wars. But had he not raised false expectations in the first place, it might have been possible to reassure the public that, for most, the risk of serious disease and death was actually quite low.

FEAR MONGERING

This trend toward fearfulness has been developing in America since well before the pandemic. For many years now, parents have been fearful about allowing their children to play without constant direct supervision. Fears of child abduction, sexual abuse, disease, peanut allergies, etc., have all been greatly exaggerated by the media and have led to overprotective parenting (Lukianoff & Haidt, 2015). As Americans, we are told what to eat to stay healthy, how much exercise is necessary, how to recycle, and that we must reduce our carbon footprint, etc. Young adults insist that "safe spaces" be created for them where they will not have to be exposed to ideas or images that frighten them. University students demand that they be warned ahead of time if topics to be discussed might potentially "trigger" them. Politicians like the ex-mayor of New York City, Michael Bloomberg, have argued that government should control our dietary input of foods that contain sugar and salt. If "woke" Progressives had their way, we would all live in a "nanny state."

The trend in society has been one of increasing authoritarian control based on the misguided notion that the state can keep us safe. Childlike illusions of perfection are being imposed on society by neurotic adults, and their greatest proponents are elites, who as a group have been psychologically "enriched" for obsessional neuroticisms, and are addicted to controlling themselves and others. (R. Kradin, 2018)

COVID-19 AND THE WITCH CRAZE

Disseminated false "narratives" have exaggerated the lethality of the virus while promoting ineffective therapeutic strategies that primarily enrich *Big Pharma* and expand the emergency powers of the central government. Through a systematic campaign of disinformation, truth has been reduced to whatever people choose to believe, regardless of facts.[43] As a result, the public is poorly informed, anxious, and prone to making bad decisions.

In a famous Depression-era radio address to the American public, President Franklin Delano Roosevelt cautioned that "We have nothing to fear but fear itself." At the time, he was lauded for encouraging the public to confront challenges with optimism. Yet when Donald Trump encouraged the American public not to be overly afraid of the virus, his remarks were widely denigrated as "insensitive."

The response to the pandemic has been polarized along political lines. Progressive Democratic voters appear to be most likely to fear the effects of COVID-19, and they have shown a willingness to accept authoritarian approaches to punishing those who choose to ignore government guidelines. In a 2021 poll, roughly half of Democratic voters favored placing non-vaccinated Americans in isolation "camps," stripping them of their civil rights, and taking away their children. Luckily, nearly all Republican and most Independent voters find such penalties unacceptable. But it appears that many once reasonable Americans have lost the ability to discern right from wrong, and are now inclined to do anything that will allay their anxiety, even if it means scapegoating their neighbors.

This is not the first time that such extraordinary fearful reactions

---

43 Arguably the vilest aspect of this campaign has been the routine claim that conservatives are pushing "disinformation" on the American public. With the assistance of big tech companies, the government has succeeded in turning the truth upside down and keeping it from public view, as it does not support their narrative.

have divided America. The need to identify a reason for the pandemic and to scapegoat one's neighbor is reminiscent of the 1692 New England witch craze. Driven by what can best be termed mass hysteria, entire towns in colonial Massachusetts and Connecticut accused innocent women, and to a lesser extent men, of bewitching young girls. Communities were thrown into a frenzied state of heightened awareness; neighbors scrutinized neighbors for evidence of wrongdoing. It required no more than innuendo for the town's elite experts—many, as today, the Harvard graduates of their time—to serve as jurists and to sentence innocent people to the gallows. (Schiff, 2015)

The parallels to what is transpiring today in America are evident. Many Americans now see their neighbors as a source of danger and as "evil." They scrutinize whether they are wearing masks or have been vaccinated and report them to authorities if they are not complying with "rules" never approved by the general public. They wish them harm and seek to punish them. It is a "witch hunt" by modern-day hysterical "puritans."

It was only when brave members of these communities refused to allow any more of their neighbors to die that the witch craze finally came to an end. But the events left the affected communities in tatters, and it took many years for the wounds to mend. One day, the present pandemic will end, and hopefully, sanity will be restored. But that will only occur when enough Americans stand up and refuse to cooperate any further with irrational pandemic "rules" set by officials. And at some point, those who succumbed to the hysteria and behaved badly will be called upon to answer for their actions, just as the elite judges of Salem, MA, were.

WUHAN

A discussion concerning the pandemic would not be complete without an examination of how it likely originated. Most experts today, with the notable exception of Drs. Fauci and Francis Collins, the Head of the NIH, think that it is most likely that Covid-9 originated in the biosafety laboratory of the Wuhan Virology Institute (WVI).

A biosafety laboratory level 4 (BSL-4), is supposed to maintain the highest level of precaution for work with infectious agents that can be aerosol-transmitted and cause fatal disease. BSL-4 laboratories are used for diagnostic testing and research on transmissible pathogens that can cause fatal disease. These include a number of viruses known to cause viral hemorrhagic fever, including the highly virulent Ebola and Marburg viruses.

Numerous precautions should be taken at these facilities. All work is done in a biosafety cabinet by personnel wearing positive pressure suits. When exiting the facility, personnel must pass through a chemical shower for decontamination, then through another room for removing positive-pressure suits, followed by a shower. Entry into a BSL-4 laboratory should be restricted to trained and authorized individuals, and all persons entering and exiting the laboratory should be monitored. BSL-4 laboratories should also be separated from areas that receive unrestricted traffic, and all laboratory waste, including filtered air, water, and trash must be thoroughly decontaminated before leaving the facility.

BSL-4 laboratories are scattered throughout the world. There are a number of BSL-4s in the US, some administered by the NIH and NIAID; one in San Antonio, Texas, is privately owned. Whereas no single federal agency is responsible for regulating these labs, US high-containment laboratories must be inspected periodically by the CDC or USDA, and they must adhere to standards as well as maintain ongoing education on biosecurity and biosafety policies.

The Wuhan Virology Institute (WVI) has existed since 1956, although its first BSL-4 facility was constructed in 2015. Past work at the Institute has involved coronaviruses that are endemic in bats. Work there has included "gain of function" research, in which the genome of a virus is modified to augment its transmission and virulence.

When an outbreak of human infection due to coronavirus occurred in China, it was initially reported that the virus had emerged from infected animals from a "wet market" located near the WVI. But some scientists were skeptical due to the reported gene sequence of SARS 2-CoV and argued that the new virus had instead been engineered by gain-of-function research and had likely escaped from the Wuhan BSL-4. The immediate response by Dr. Fauci and the media to these claims was to deny them and to label such ideas as "misinformation" and instead to insist that the virus had evolved naturally. But despite substantial efforts, no one was able to explain changes in the genome sequence that had no precursor in nature, nor were they able to identify an infected intermediate host. Bats were not sold at the nearby wet market, and the closest bat caves were hundreds of miles away, making natural transmission unlikely.

Dr. Steven Quay, an expert in molecular biology examined the sequences of SARS-CoV2:

> The purpose of the analysis was to determine the origin of SARS-CoV-2, the virus that causes COVID-19. Beginning with a likelihood of 98.2 percent that it was a zoonotic jump from nature with only a 1.2 percent probability it was a laboratory escape, twenty-six different, independent facts and evidence were examined systematically. The final conclusion is that it is a 99.8 percent probability SARS-CoV-2 came from a laboratory and only a 0.2 percent likelihood it came from nature. (Quay, 2021)[44]

---

44 Steve Quay and I were pathology residents together in the late 1970s, and I know him to be a rigorous scientist who enjoys getting at truths that are being covered up.

When Dr. Fauci's internal e-mails became public, it was evident that there had been early suspicion amongst scientists that the virus had been bioengineered, and that Fauci together with Dr. Francis Collins, the head of the NIH, had made concerted efforts to discredit them and to have them withdraw their initial assessments. Testifying before Congress, Fauci denied that "gain of function" research had taken place, although the NIH subsequently admitted that it had funded such research at WVI, raising the real possibility that Fauci purposefully lied to Congress. (Opinion, 2021)

While denying that it had contributed to the creation of SARS-CoV2, the NIH did reveal that coronavirus experimentation had been funded at WVI through a US-based nonprofit in 2018 and 2019 and that this had led to the "unexpected result" of creating a coronavirus that was more infectious in mice.

> NIH said that the organization holding the parent grant, the EcoHealth Alliance, had failed to report this result to the agency, as required. A newly released progress report on that grant also shows that EcoHealth and WIV conducted experiments changing the virus that causes Middle East respiratory syndrome (MERS), which is raising additional questions. NIH noted in its letter that when the agency reviewed the original EcoHealth grant proposal, it determined the proposed experiments—designed to determine whether certain bat coronaviruses might infect humans—did not meet its definition of so-called gain-of-function (GOF) experiments that can make pathogens more dangerous to humans…. Critics of NIH who claim the agency has lied about the work it funded at WIV pounced on the letter. Rutgers University, Piscataway, microbiologist Richard Enright, a prominent critic of GOF research, commented in a tweet, "NIH corrects untruthful assertions by NIH Director [Francis] Collins and NIAID [National Institute of Allergy and Infectious Diseases] Director [Anthony] Fauci that NIH had not funded gain-of-function research in Wuhan." …Claims that the US government helped fund research into coronaviruses spread after the *Daily Mail* reported it obtained documents that "show the

Wuhan Institute of Virology undertook coronavirus experiments on mammals captured more than 1,000 miles away in Yunnan – funded by a \$3.7 million grant from the US government." ...In 2014, the NIH approved a grant to EcoHealth Alliance designated for research into "Understanding the Risk of Bat Coronavirus Emergence." The project involved collaborating with researchers at the Wuhan Institute of Virology to study coronaviruses in bats and the risk of potential transfer to humans. (Editor, 2021)

The likelihood that the US assisted in funding "gain of function" research in China that led to the current pandemic should trouble every American. It suggests both hubris and dishonesty on the part of scientists at the NIH. Its close relationships with China appear to have caused it to turn a blind eye to the fact that the CCP is a competitor, a country where human rights have little import, and a potential military foe of the US. It ignored the likelihood that safety protocols in China would be carried out with less rigor than in the West and continues to put the world at risk for future and possibly more deadly pandemics. It is distressing to realize that there are ambitious American scientists and entrepreneurs who are of the mindset that, if technology can achieve it and there are profits to be had, then "everything is permissible."

BIOTERRORISM

Americans tend to be naïve. They find it difficult to think the worst of others and historically have been slow to react to threats. Indeed, it is part of the Progressive/utopian mindset to be optimistic on the topic of human nature. It took America years to enter both World War I and World War II, although it was clear that German ambitions posed a threat to the Free World. Unlike Churchill, Roosevelt was unwilling to view Stalin as a threat, and as a result, much of Eastern Europe was consigned to life behind the "Iron Curtain" of Communism for forty years. So what can be said about the CCP's unleashing of COVID-19? Was it an honest mistake? An undeclared act of war? A bioterrorist attack?

In *21 Lessons for the 21st Century*, the Israeli historian Yuval Noah Hariri argues that:

Terrorists are masters of mind control. They kill very few people but nevertheless manage to terrify billions and rattle huge structures such as the European Union or the United States. (Hariri, 2018)

When the coronavirus was first noted in Wuhan, the CCP had a decision to make. In the past, when outbreaks of infection occurred from its wet markets, China acted promptly to control the spread of infection and alerted the outside world to the potential threat. But it did not do this in the winter of 2019/20. Instead, it took austere efforts to lock down the infection in China, while allowing infected people from Wuhan to travel to Europe and the United States, thereby virtually assuring that the virus would spread, which it did. It failed to inform the world that the virus was airborne, virtually ensuring that a pandemic would ensue. Instead, the CCP made efforts to buy up much of the world's supply of protective personal equipment (PPE) and falsified images of people dying on the streets of Wuhan specifically to stoke fear. In the current atmosphere of "woke" culture, to suggest that the CCP purposefully initiated the COVID-19 pandemic would be viewed as "dark" and "racist" by many. Certainly, Progressives have repeatedly shown that they have no appetite for confronting unpleasantness if it conflicts with their preferred narratives.

But there is good reason to conclude that the actions of the CCP were nefarious. While, admittedly, we do not, and may never know exactly what the CCP was up to in the winter of 2019, its actions say everything. We *know* that the virus emerged from China and that *no* effort was made to contain it from the outside world. We *know* that the CCP has refused to cooperate with efforts of experts in the West to ascertain the source of the virus.

One need not identify a "smoking gun." to assess what the CCP likely had in mind. In 2019, China was facing economic challenges, and the likely re-election of Donald Trump, who unlike his predecessors, had made concerted and successful efforts at limiting China's economic and military expansion. His imposition of tariffs on Chinese exports created a strain on China's economic growth and threatened the CCP's long-range plans for world hegemony. Whether one terms SARS-CoV2 a weapon of biological warfare or an example bioterrorism hardly matters, as the desired effects were the same. As Hariri states on the topic of terrorism:

> Following an act of terrorism, the enemy has the same number of soldiers, tanks, and ships as before. The enemy's communication network, roads, and railways are largely intact. His factories, ports, and bases remain untouched. However, the terrorists hope that even though they can barely make a dent in the enemy's material power, fear and confusion will cause the enemy to misuse his intact strength and overreact ...In this respect, terrorists resemble a fly that tries to destroy a china shop ...How does a fly destroy a China shop? It finds a bull, gets inside its ear and starts buzzing. The bull goes wild with fear and anger, and destroys the china shop. (Hariri, 2018)

It is no stretch of the imagination to liken America to the "bull" and China to the "fly" in this scenario. The "china shop" was our economic, political, and educational system.

Consider the effects of the Wuhan virus. A previously booming American economy is witnessing the highest inflation rate in forty years. A confrontational American President, who was a thorn in the side of the CCP, has been replaced by a cognitively-challenged weak one, who may well be compromised by financial ties to the CCP. American children have been unable to attend school for more than a year and most remain behind unnecessary masks, and American society is more culturally and politically polarized than ever. Could things have worked out better for the CCP, the corporate globalists, or the Democratic party, all of which would like to impose a new authoritarian world order? I think not.

America is now divided between those who have successfully metabolized their fear of COVID-19 versus those who either will not or cannot. Dr. Fauci and his supporters have warned that Americans may have to accept receiving "booster" injections against COVID-19 every several months, with no end in sight. It should have been evident to medical professionals that the pandemic was being mishandled, yet most remained silent concerning this uncomfortable truth. In the next chapter, we will consider why physicians did not act to put the pandemic into proper perspective. But for clarity, I have summarized the takeaway key points of the COVID-19 pandemic below:

SUMMARY OF THE COVID-19 PANDEMIC

- SARS-2 Corona virus-2019 (COVID-19) is a novel coronavirus, *likely* genetically engineered in a Chinese laboratory, and *definitely* cynically unleashed on the world.

- The vast majority of severe illness and death occur in the elderly (>70 years of age) with multiple recognized risk factors (obesity, cardiopulmonary disease, diabetes, high blood pressure, immunosuppression).

- The risk of dying from coronavirus infection is estimated at ~1 percent if you are elderly, and perhaps as high as 8 percent if you have multiple risk factors and are already flirting with death. It is less than 0.15 percent if you are a young and otherwise healthy adult.

- Unfortunately, genuinely accurate mortality rates do not exist because record-keeping has been both inconsistent and flawed.

- Deaths are primarily due to severe viral pneumonia and multi-organ failure.

- Young children *rarely* develop severe infection or die from COVID-19 and are ineffective spreaders of the virus.

- Most disease is spread by those with active signs of infection.

- The ability of asymptomatic infected individuals to spread the infection is likely low but has not been accurately ascertained.

- Mask-wearing by the general public with non-N95 masks is ineffective at protecting against contracting or spreading coronavirus. *There is no justification for mask mandates.*

- Social distancing *does not* reduce the risk of viral spread in a population.

- The chance of becoming infected when socially distanced *outside* is *essentially nil.*

- There is no evidence that lockdowns have been effective.

- Lockdowns delay achieving "herd immunity" and may select for potentially more virulent stains of coronavirus.

- The deleterious economic, social, and health consequences of lockdowns have been substantial.

- The new DNA and mRNA vaccines against COVID-19 *may* be protective against severe illness and death in 65–90 percent of people, but this number is uncertain due to the emergence of mutated variants.

- The current vaccines do not appear to limit either becoming infected or spreading infection with mutant variants.

- There is no evidence that "boosters" limit the severity of disease.

- The potential long-term risks of the mRNA and DNA vaccine strategies exceed those seen with standard vaccines but have not been assessed.

- Mutated COVID-19 variants represent an unpredictable risk for both the vaccinated and unvaccinated.

- The omicron variant has not convincingly been shown to be dangerous for those who have either recovered from COVID-19 or have been vaccinated.

- There is a good chance that the pandemic is currently moving toward becoming endemic.

- The pandemic has been driven primarily by fear and misinformation fed to us by our nation's public health experts.
- Americans are becoming increasingly neurotic and willing to divest themselves of their freedoms.

The following codicils are noteworthy:

1. Medicine is not an exact science, nor does it necessarily follow the rules that most would describe as rational.

2. The available information concerning COVID-19 has been distorted by the press, politicians, and health professionals to fit a narrative, making it all but impossible to make accurate statements about the pandemic.

3. Respiratory viral diseases are difficult to treat and almost impossible to eliminate.

4. Death is an unavoidable aspect of life, and not unexpectedly affects the aged and sick disproportionately.

CHAPTER FIVE: COVID-19 AND THE MEDICAL PROFESSION

Whoever in the pursuit of science seeks after immediate practical utility may generally rest assured that he will seek in vain.

—Hermann van Helmholz

MEDICINE AS SCIENCE?

Before attending medical school, I earned a master's degree in chemical physics, an experience that left me with an appreciation for the precision of the physical sciences.

In medical school, I recognized that there were important differences between the medical and physical sciences. The conduct of most experiments in physics and chemistry involves small numbers of variables that can be tightly controlled. In addition, most experiments can be repeated many times, and results are measured by highly accurate instruments. A well-performed set of experiments can yield results differing by at most a few places after the decimal point.

This is not true of medical experiments, including drug trials. The reason is easily grasped. An animal cell is complex; it has been estimated to contain ~42 million protein molecules, not accounting for DNA, RNA, fat, and carbohydrates that are also present. Science has only scratched the surface of the interactions taking place within the cell. When one considers the human body, which is comprised of ~15 trillion cells, it should be obvious that the difficulties in attempting to determine the accuracy of a response to a drug are greater than those encountered in measuring the boiling point of water. When one contemplates this, it is extraordinary that we know as much as we do about how the body functions.

But it is as likely that our current state of scientific knowledge is flawed. History teaches us that science is always in flux. In the *Structure of Scientific Revolutions*, Thomas Kuhn described how reigning scientific paradigms tend to undergo deconstruction and replacement by new ones (Kuhn, 1962). In addition, the scientific approach to nature appears to be dependent on scale. For hundreds of years, Newton's mechanics were thought to be the last word in the physics of how bodies move in time and space, until the discovery of quantum mechanics replaced them with a more accurate description. Whereas we still use Newton's equations to solve problems in the visible world, quantum mechanics is required to explain events that occur at the atomic level. Simple systems can be described in terms of linear cause-and-effect models. But these do not apply to complex systems, where other forms of mathematics are necessary.

Medical science has never developed what might be termed an overarching paradigm, but what we know has been primarily on linear approaches to cause and effect. But as the human body is highly complex, it is likely that our current perspectives on medicine are at best poor approximations.

What then can reasonably be expected of medical experimentation? The answer is results with a high—and arguably unacceptable—degree of variability. While some physiological activities do behave in a predictable linear manner (e.g., the hormone epinephrine will reliably speed the heart's rate and contractility, and acetylsalicylic acid [aspirin] will reduce the body temperature of a feverish patient), many biological activities are too complex to predict. We know little as to what causes polygenetic chronic diseases such as obesity, arthritis, etc., and even less about how to treat them.

To the case in point, it is virtually impossible to predict how an individual will respond to being infected with COVID-19 or to a therapeutic or to a vaccine that targets the virus. Interpreting experimental findings can be difficult, as the current pandemic has demonstrated. Whereas we can suggest in a crude manner how a population may respond, all bets are off when considering the responses of individuals. Admittedly, there are philosophically liberal scientists who would label this a "dark" perspective on medical science, but again ideology has no place in these arguments. What counts is what best fits the observed data.

CLINICAL TRIALS

In most clinical trials in which new drugs or vaccines are tested for their efficacy, studies are conducted on large randomly chosen groups, with placebo controls. The randomized controlled trial (RCT) was introduced in the 1950s, and it only became the standard of clinical trial testing for the FDA in the mid-1970s. Prior to that, assessing drug efficacy was based primarily on *anecdotal* evidence.

As I discussed in *The Placebo Response,* conclusions concerning therapeutic efficacy for groups cannot be assessed based on the anecdotal responses of individuals under uncontrolled circumstances (R. Kradin, 2008). While anecdotal responses may appear convincing, they may fail to hold up under controlled conditions with large numbers of subjects. There are a number of reasons for this, including subject diversity, changes in test conditions, the phenomenon of regression to the "mean,"[45] etc.; unfortunately, a detailed discussion is beyond the scope of the present text.

Consider the controversy concerning the efficacy of HCQ as a treatment for coronavirus infection. Physicians and numerous patients

---

45 Regression to the mean was described by the mathematician Francis Galton (Charles Darwin's cousin). As the tendency for repeated measurements to move toward a mean value. This is why physicians are taught to take multiple blood pressure determinations at different times before starting a patient on a blood pressure medication, because this will provide the most accurate answer.

who received HCQ were convinced that it reduces the severity of coronavirus symptoms and saves lives. Despite what Dr. Fauci and many in the medical profession argued, HCQ had been used safely for a century for the treatment of malaria and certain autoimmune diseases, and for all intents and purposes, it is as safe as most drugs get. The CDC said as much on its website:

> Hydroxychloroquine can be prescribed to adults and children of all ages. It can also be safely taken by pregnant women and nursing mothers.... CDC has no limits on the use of hydroxychloroquine for the prevention of malaria. When hydroxychloroquine is used at higher doses for many years, a rare eye condition called retinopathy has occurred. ("Hydroxychloroquine," 2021)

Deaths are virtually unheard of except in those who have either taken excessive amounts of the drug or have underlying cardiac disease. Thus, even if the drug were to prove ineffective, the risk-to-benefit ratio for administering HCQ to patients with Covid-19 is also *very* low in critically ill patients with few other treatment options was reasonable.

Yet, academic medical scientists were outspoken in their skepticism of HCQ and felt their criticism was justified when some RCTs failed to show efficacy. But other studies showed that HCQ had beneficial results in early infection. A meta-analysis that examined the available studies did not find a definite benefit for HCQ, but the authors admitted that the level of confidence for their conclusion was low (Ebina-Shibuya, Namkoong, Horita & al, 2021). So, what *is* the correct answer?

To approach the issue, one must recognize that there is always a potential discrepancy between effects seen in individuals and those observed in controlled trials. In virtually every RCT, there are individuals who show good responses that may not be representative of the group as a whole. Does that mean that the individual who benefitted imagined the effects? No, it does not.

Take the initial RCT of the drug gefitinib, an epidermal growth factor receptor EGFR-inhibitor used to treat lung cancer. In that trial, the drug showed no efficacy for the group compared to controls. But investigators recognized that there had been patients who had substantial anti-tumor responses. When they examined these responders in greater detail, they found that their tumors showed specific mutations in the EGFR gene that were not seen in non-responders. When the drug was retested in patients whose tumors had the EGFR mutation versus placebo control, it proved highly effective, and it is now first-line treatment for the 20 percent of lung adenocarcinoma patients whose tumors harbor an EGFR mutation.

Might there be an underlying genetic trait in patients with COVID-19s who responded well to HCQ? It is possible, but we will likely never know because researchers are unlikely to pursue the answer. For unlike gefitinib, which was a novel innovative drug that stood to make or lose millions for its pharmaceutical developer, HCQ is cheap and no longer on patent, so its widespread use will not result in huge profits. The use of HCQ to treat COVID-19 was strongly condemned by Dr. Fauci and much of the medical profession, and Donald Trump suggesting its possible efficacy was enough for many to ridicule and seek to ban it. But that's economics and politics; it's *not* science.

There has been a general trend in medicine toward personalizing treatments based on individual genetic profiles and other personal variables. For Fauci and others to insist that everyone receive a vaccination against COVID-19, in a one size fits all approach without consideration of an individual's medical history, flies in the face of the direction that medical science has been moving for the last thirty years.[46]

---

46 There has been a definite trend towards "personalized medicine" in which individual aspects of a patient's biology and genetics determine the direction of treatment. This is especially true in "targeted" cancer treatments, but also occurs regularly in other areas of medicine. The idea of treating all individuals identically defies medical progress and suggests how out of touch or duplicitous Dr. Fauci and his colleagues have been in recommending vaccination mandates for all.

MODELING DISEASE

Unlike epidemiologists, who are scientists that investigate the causes of disease based on the study of large populations, most physicians treat individuals. Epidemiologists have a good deal of experience with infectious diseases, but their predictions concerning pandemics are often based on mathematical modeling that can be inaccurate. The early prediction of the number of individuals in the US likely to die from COVID-19 was based on mathematical modeling by a research group at Oxford University.

> Governments across the world are relying on mathematical projections to help guide decisions in this pandemic. Computer simulations account for only a fraction of the data analyses that modeling teams have performed in the crisis, Ferguson notes, but they are an increasingly important part of policymaking. But, as he and other modelers warn, much information about how SARS-CoV-2 spreads is still unknown and must be estimated or assumed—and that limits the precision of forecasts. An earlier version of the Imperial model, for instance, estimated that SARS-CoV-2 would be about as severe as influenza in necessitating the hospitalization of those infected. That turned out to be incorrect. (Adam, 2020)

The Oxford Group estimated that over two million in the US would die, more than twice the current number of deaths. These predictions were based on linear modeling, which is inappropriate when applied to complex systems that do not behave in a linear manner. Physicists today recognize that complex systems require mathematical approaches that can describe *chaos*. This may explain, in part, why modeling the pandemic failed to predict its behavior accurately. An example of a chaotic system is the weather, and this is why short-term weather forecasting is often accurate, but it is virtually impossible to predict weather patterns over the course of weeks, months, or years. And if we cannot predict the weather a month from now, how accurate might scientific predictions be concerning even more complex phenomena, such as "global warming?"[47] There is a need for far more humility amongst scientists.

But something more concerning occurred during the pandemic with regard to disease modeling. Some researchers failed to revise their modeling predictions based on the *actual* occurrence of cases. The point of disease modeling is to make initial predictions and then to modify them based on "facts on the ground." If that does not happen, the model becomes unhinged from reality, and that is not in keeping with science. Indeed, the history of science in the modern era has been based on revising theories in the face of unexplained observations. Based on careful measurements of planetary motion, the heliocentric model of Copernicus replaced the old Ptolemaic system, and the modern scientific age began.

ARE PHYSICIANS SCIENTISTS?

We tend to think of physicians as scientists. But that's not precisely accurate. While having studied science as part of their preliminary training, most physicians are not actively engaged in scientific research. The current trend in academic medicine to develop physician-researchers with MD-PhDs neglects to consider that excellent research, like excellent medical practice, is almost always a full-time endeavor. For this reason, physician-researchers who attempt to straddle both roles, despite impressive qualifications, often prove to be mediocre at both of their roles.

Most physicians are skilled professionals with a background in

---

47 I am not a climate denier. I recognize that there is good evidence that the climate is warming. But that is not the same as concluding that the use of carbon products is the major or only reason for the change. Nor does it imply that the change will be irreversible in the next several years or that America reducing its carbon footprint when polluters like China and India do not is likely to make an impact on the phenomenon. But to say these things is considered heinous by some on the Progressive Left.

medical science, experience with treating disease, and hopefully at least a modicum of common sense. With rare exception, they are not virologists, immunologists, or pharmacologists, and it is wrong to expect expertise from them on all these subjects. Unfortunately, since the onset of the present pandemic, many have consistently ignored the available scientific evidence, refused to learn from clinical experience, and regrettably displayed less than the required amount of common sense.

It is distressing to hear Dr. Fauci drone on about how it is critical that we all "follow the science," or worse to suggest that he "represents science," as he has done. Instead of maintaining scientific standards, he has repeatedly ignored scientific evidence with respect to the efficacy of masks, lockdowns, therapeutics, and the importance of acquired immunity (S. Atlas, 2021). Fauci's insistence that *all* decision-making be made based on carefully designed and conducted RCTs is disingenuous, especially as the RCT used to approve Remdesivir, which he approved, was deeply flawed by all accounts. While it is admirable for the medical profession to seek to appear *scientific*, it is foolhardy to imagine that the findings of RCTs are as accurate as some have claimed. Any physician who insists on viewing medicine as irrefutable science, instead of what it really is, which is an open-ended and at times chaotic search for truth, does not understand the field.

When I lecture on the placebo response, I often query audiences as to whether they can tell me how many glasses of red wine are good for you or if eating red meat is a bad thing? If they are old enough, they have heard and read many contradictory opinions on these questions. The reason is that the variables involved in determining the answer are so complex that no matter how many times clinical trials are performed, different answers are obtained. The press and the ill-informed run with the most recently published *answer* for a time until another study comes along that refutes it.

Many factors go into determining whether statistical significance will be achieved in a randomized controlled drug trial. First, the number of subjects in a trial must be large enough to get a clear signal as to the outcome. The presence of large numbers of "placebo responders" makes it more difficult to detect significant differences between groups. This has been especially true for some psychiatric disorders, e.g., anxiety and depression, where placebo effects are for uncertain reasons often high.

Another well-recognized phenomenon in the world of clinical trials is that initial results are often better than those subsequently observed. Case in point: the likelihood that the new vaccines for COVID-19 would prove to be greater than 95 percent effective was low, and we now know that they are not—and apparently far from it. In fact, a careful examination of the data by the FDA would have revealed that the interpretation of the initial vaccine results from these studies was exaggerated.

Don't all physicians know this? I would venture to say that most do not. The average physician is understandably primarily interested in finding treatments for his patients and less concerned with the science of how to interpret data from clinical trials or the science of placebos. Most have not spent their career doing any form of research, and they are not engaged in critiquing detailed scientific research. Rather, they take their cues from medical experts and medical societies, as most have in the present pandemic. Unfortunately, scientific research is also arguably less rigorous today than in the past, as it has been eroded by economic, political, and cultural influences. There is an increasing tendency in society-at-large to allow bias to influence how research data is interpreted.

MEDICINE AND THE PRIVATE SECTOR

"Operation Warp Speed" showed what the private sector can do in cooperation with the Federal Government. Donald Trump's inclination to move things rapidly along by undoing regulatory roadblocks may have paid off. After all, it was virtually unheard of to develop a vaccine, meet FDA approval, and bring it to market in less than a year. But there is reason to doubt whether the grand effort was a stellar success, as we currently know that the available vaccines are less than optimal. What we do know is that they are not behaving as vaccines are supposed to and that they have had some serious untoward side effects.

In the rush to reduce the inflated fears surrounding the virus, the medical profession was too eager to accept that the new vaccines would keep us safe. At times, one must be prepared to throw out all previous conceptions and start the evaluation process all over again. This is something that our health experts and politicians have been unwilling to do. Instead, they have chosen to cling to any part of their scientific narrative that hasn't yet been fully discredited, that is until it is.

THE DIRECTION OF MEDICAL SCIENCE

Much of the recent progress in medical science has been technological, rather than conceptual, and has resulted from the work of bio- and molecular engineers. We have far more accurate radiographic imaging, as well as new blood and molecular tests to detect disease. With the assistance of computers, we can now analyze a great deal more data than ever before.

Unfortunately, medical education has not yet come to grips with the challenges posed by the amount of information that needs to be processed in the field of medicine. It is no longer possible for a physician to know all that he needs to know, as the human mind can only store so much information. Having a veritable mountain of informa-tion at one's fingertips on a computer or on the Internet is convenient, but it is not the same as processing and storing information in your own mind, where it can interact in ways that are beneficial. It is fair to say that physicians have grown excessively reliant on sources outside themselves for their decision-making.

If medical education is to be limited to four years of schooling, educators need to make critical choices as to what will and will not be taught. Most medical schools base their curricula on trends set by the prestigious front-runners in the field—medical schools like Harvard, Yale, and Johns Hopkins. These institutions are all Progressive in their orientation, and as such, they insist on placing more value on what is "new" versus "old." For example, the autopsy, once a staple for teach-ing and hospital quality control, has virtually disappeared because it is viewed as "antiquated" and is also not a lucrative procedure, despite the fact that it continues to identify major diagnoses that are often missed during life in up to a quarter of hospital deaths.

Today's medical students spend considerable time learning about new genetic and molecular advances, although many of these findings are not ready for "prime time" and have little direct bearing on clinical care. This focus on what's new and "exciting" comes at the expense of learning how to do a competent physical examination, taking a detailed medical history, and studying the spectrum of pathologies that a physi-cian is likely to encounter in practice.

As a result of living in the rapidly changing digital age, cognitive decision-making processes have been forced to keep pace, and are now so rapid as to preclude the possibility of pondering complex challenges. When faced with treating common diseases, most young physicians today are competent, but when confronted with unusual cases, they may have little idea how to approach them. As medical education has increasingly become an extension of the Progressive education in universities, young physicians today are spending more time focusing on social justice advocacy than on the nuts and bolts of medical practice.

In academic centers, a growing percentage of trainees have combined MD-PhD degrees in the basic sciences. This has resulted in a substantial shift toward approaching patients like scientific experiments. In my experience, many of these physicians lack common sense and fail to appreciate that scientific rigor cannot be achieved in medical practice. In my experience, nowhere in clinical medicine is this truer than in the field of infectious disease.

INFECTIOUS DISEASE SPECIALISTS

In my years as a pulmonary physician and pathologist, I worked closely with infectious disease doctors, including Dr. Walensky. I have authored several standard texts on the pathology of infectious diseases (R. Kradin, 2017) including one devoted to respiratory viruses (Fraire, 'Woda, Kradin, & al, 2016). I held my infectious disease colleagues in high esteem, for as a rule, they were intelligent, thorough, and unlikely to leave "stones unturned" in their quest to make a diagnosis or formulate an effective treatment. But they were also inclined to be *overly* rigorous. Their decision-making was invariably dependent on data, and like Dr. Fauci, they tended to denigrate anecdotal evidence. Consequently, their clinical advice could be overly cautious. More than other medical specialists, they tended to be risk averse. From a purely scientific perspective, it was hard to fault their approach, but medicine, as I have argued, currently is not a rigorous science, and it was often necessary to ignore their recommendations and treat patients' problems with a substantial dose of common sense.

For these reasons, it may not be entirely by chance that the approach taken by our public health experts has been cautious in the extreme, as in the absence of unequivocal data, they have been unwilling to make commonsensical decisions. "Perfectionism" has not allowed them to admit that there are no perfect scientific answers to the current pandemic. As a result, the public is suffering from the neuroticisms of our public health leaders, with economic and political interests further confounding matters.

Anthony Fauci, MD

The advice of Dr. Anthony Fauci on how to control the pandemic has been a source of distress for some, although Progressives have tended to place him on an undeserved pedestal, more for his political bias than his scientific prowess. Fauci has been a fixture at the NIH for more than half a century, and he continues at the helm of America's public health response, at an age when most have retired gracefully. What many Americans do not know is that Fauci is neither an infectious disease expert nor is he an epidemiologist. His area of expertise is clinical immunology, and he earned his reputation in the area of HIV/AIDS research.

Fauci's tenure at NIH has been controversial and he has a reputation for being petty and vindictive. He is the highest-paid public official in the US Government, earning more than $400,000 annually, with an estimated net worth of more than ten million dollars (Kennedy Jr., 2021). In *The Real Anthony Fauci*, Robert Kennedy Jr. details Fauci's long checkered history of working closely with *Big Pharma* and the Gates Foundation, especially in the arena of vaccine development.

Laymen do not always appreciate that prestigious positions in medicine are no different than politicians in government. The political physician is not usually the most clinically competent. The elite in society in their naivete too often equate competence with being the department "head." But it is more often the lowly "clinical instructor" who has been practicing his craft for years without the diversion of having to direct a laboratory, write research grants, or administer a department, who is best positioned to provide excellent medical care.

Arguably the greatest error of the Trump Presidency was appointing Fauci to head the Coronavirus Task Force. His recommendations were consistently wrong. In addition, he repeatedly passive-aggressively undermined Trump's credibility. For this, Progressives and "Never Trumpers" elevated him to saintly status, ignoring the fact that his counsel was inconsistent and incorrect.

There is no evidence that he followed the evolving scientific data, and he has been steadfast in his unwillingness to be held responsible or accountable for his mishaps and their consequences for the public. Despite repeated denials while giving Congressional testimony, there can be little doubt that he was aware that the current virus was likely engineered. His agenda has been personal and political.

Fauci was joined by Dr. Deborah Birx, a physician and "diplomat" as Wikipedia describes her, who served as the Government's primary "epidemiologist" during the Trump administration, and who was also often wrong on important matters. Birx is an immunologist who worked in Fauci's NIH laboratory in the past. After Biden's election, she was openly critical of Trump's handling of the pandemic but remained mum on the matter while serving in Trump's administration. Dr. Rochelle Walensky, the current head of the CDC, is an infectious disease specialist who worked primarily on HIV/AIDS and had recently been appointed the head of Infectious Disease at Massachusetts General Hospital before being tapped by Fauci and the Biden administration to head the CDC. So the theme emerges of Fauci having picked physicians who shared his interest in HIV/AIDS to head up the public health response to coronavirus. Unfortunately, although both are viruses, HIV and SARS-CoV2 have little in common, and knowledge concerning a sexually-transmitted slowly progressive disease has little relevance for how to approach a pandemic due to a virulent respiratory virus.

These health experts have been in denial of the deleterious effects of lockdowns on other medical conditions, due to patients fearing to go to the hospital for tests and treatment. They have ignored the mental health consequences of closing schools, including increased anxiety, depression, and suicidality, in the face of overwhelming scientific evidence that disease does not negatively affect the young.

Emergency room visits for adolescent suicide attempts soared this past summer and winter, especially among girls, perhaps in connection with America's struggles with COVID-19, new Centers for Disease Control and Prevention data revealed Friday.

There was a 22.3 percent spike in ER trips for children aged 12 to 17 in summer 2020 compared to 2019, according to findings published in the CDC's "Morbidity and Mortality Weekly Report."

That trend seemed to continue into this recently completed academic year, as visits were up by 39.1 percent this winter, compared to the previous winter, the report said. (Li, 2021)

The CDC has pandered to the demands of the National Educational Association, the teachers union, whose members have apparently been too afraid to return to work, and who have shown an absence of concern for the welfare of their students.

Recently, when challenged by Senator Rand Paul about the soundness of his health recommendations, Fauci failed to answer coherently but was unfazed. He has adamantly denied any role in funding gain of function research at the Wuhan facility, despite acknowledgment by the NIH that it did so. When asked by Senator Lindsay Graham as to why he was troubled about America coming out of lockdown too quickly but not in the least bothered by the influx of COVID-19 positive immigrants coming across the Southern Border, Fauci simply replied that America's Southern Border is not his "concern." He gave a similar pass to the protests that followed the death of George Floyd in the summer of 2020, at the height of the pandemic. Apparently, certain political agendas trump public health policy and aren't required to "follow the science."

Dr. Fauci has much to answer for, and hopefully, someday he will. As Kennedy suggests, his strategy of suggesting that the "sky is falling" has for many years allowed him to accrue large levels of funding to the NIAID, heightened his public profile, and consolidated his power at NIH (Kennedy Jr., 2021). There are credible medical experts who see Fauci as the greatest hindrance to our ability to emerge from the current pandemic, and who would be pleased to see him removed from his current position as head of Coronavirus Task Force. But that is unlikely to happen, as long as the Biden administration sees political benefit in prolonging the pandemic. Indeed, Dr. Fauci is once again fear-mongering about the potential dangers of the new omicron coronavirus variant and floating the possibility of renewed lockdowns, mask mandates, and booster vaccinations, all in the lead-up to the 2022 mid-term elections.

Thankfully, there are physicians who have openly taken issue with the decisions that have been made by our public health experts, and they have attempted to make their voices heard. Dr. Scott Atlas from Stanford, Dr. Marty Makary of Johns Hopkins, and Robert Malone, who helped develop the technology for the new vaccines, have been high-profile vocal critics of how the pandemic has been handled. The co-signers of the *Great Barrington Declaration* include epidemiologists and infectious disease experts who object to the current health policies. Nearly one million physicians and scientists, myself included, are co-signatories. The *Declaration* reads as follows:

> The Great Barrington Declaration – As infectious disease epidemiologists and public health scientists we have grave concerns about

the damaging physical and mental health impacts of the prevailing COVID-19 policies, and recommend an approach we call Focused Protection.

Coming from both the left and right, and around the world, we have devoted our careers to protecting people. Current lockdown policies are producing devastating effects on short and long-term public health. The results (to name a few) include lower childhood vaccination rates, worsening cardiovascular disease outcomes, fewer cancer screenings and deteriorating mental health—leading to greater excess mortality in years to come, with the working class and younger members of society carrying the heaviest burden. Keeping students out of school is a grave injustice.

Keeping these measures in place until a vaccine is available will cause irreparable damage, with the underprivileged disproportionately harmed.

Fortunately, our understanding of the virus is growing. We know that vulnerability to death from COVID-19 is more than a thousand-fold higher in the old and infirm than the young. Indeed, for children, COVID-19 is less dangerous than many other harms, including influenza.

As immunity builds in the population, the risk of infection to all—including the vulnerable—falls. We know that all populations will eventually reach herd immunity—i.e. the point at which the rate of new infections is stable— and that this can be assisted by (but is not dependent upon) a vaccine. Our goal should therefore be to minimize mortality and social harm until we reach herd immunity.

The most compassionate approach that balances the risks and benefits of reaching herd immunity, is to allow those who are at minimal risk of death to live their lives normally to build up immunity to the virus through natural infection, while better protecting those who are at highest risk. We call this Focused Protection.

Adopting measures to protect the vulnerable should be the central aim of public health responses to COVID-19. By way of example, nursing homes should use staff with acquired immunity and perform frequent testing of other staff and all visitors. Staff rotation should be minimized. Retired people living at home should have groceries and other essentials delivered to their home. When possible, they should meet family members outside rather than inside. A comprehensive and detailed list of measures, including approaches to multi-generational households, can be implemented, and is well within the scope and capability of public health professionals.

Those who are not vulnerable should immediately be allowed to resume life as normal. Simple hygiene measures, such as hand washing and staying home when sick should be practiced by everyone to reduce the herd immunity threshold. Schools and universities should be open for in-person teaching. Extracurricular activities, such as sports, should be resumed. Young low-risk adults should work normally, rather than from home. Restaurants and other businesses should open. Arts, music, sport and other cultural activities should resume. People who are more at risk may participate if they wish, while society as a whole enjoys the protection conferred upon the vulnerable by those who have built up herd immunity.

Despite being a scientifically sound statement on the pandemic, and one well worthy of consideration, the authors of the *Declaration* have been subjected to withering criticisms by government health leaders and the media. A recent critique by a Progressive Professor of Medicine concluded that the *Declaration* was overly concerned with the rights of the "individual" with "insufficient concern" shown for those perceived as vulnerable groups in society. This is the standard "woke" narrative of the Left, which lauds fictional notions of victimized groups while viewing itself as "morally superior" to those who espouse dissenting views. The critique includes a gratuitous reference to Trump, i.e., a "dog whistle" for the Progressive base, and concludes that the *Declaration* should be censored:

The *Great Barrington Declaration*, supported by US President Donald Trump, is naive and dangerous. Physicians and scientists must be responsible in our pronouncements and not sow mistrust of effective public health measures. (Archer, 2020)

But the American public is becoming wise to the political agenda of the Left and its inept handling of the pandemic. Yet the question remains: why do a large portion of physicians choose to ignore science and adopt cultural narratives that are potentially harmful to public health? In order to understand this, it is necessary to place physicians "on the couch" and analyze the "root causes."

PART III

CHAPTER SIX: WHO ARE AMERICA'S PHYSICIANS?

They that are whole need not a physician…

—Matthew 9:12

To gain insight into America's medical elite, it is first necessary to understand how Progressivism has affected the educational process. Since the early twentieth century, Progressive ideas have had a profound influence on public education. John Dewey, a leading figure in America's Progressive movement, argued that government and public education were the rightful realms of an educated elite. Dewey's ideas were popularized and today, it is virtually impossible for someone schooled in America to have escaped Progressive ideological indoctrination.

In *The Age of Entitlement,* the social critic Christopher Caldwell suggests that those born in America at the beginning of the "Baby Boom"(1946–64) received a very different education than those born after the mid-1950s. The early "Boomers" received a positive perspective on America. Notions of America as "systemically racist" were never considered. Instead, a streak of patriotism ran through the educational system. The Pledge of Allegiance was recited at the beginning of each school day, with reference to America as "under God." [48]

Public education embraced post-Enlightenment liberalism, with freedom of speech, no matter how unpopular as an inviolable right.[49] History was taught in a linear fashion, and historical facts were appropriately considered within the context of their times. Columbus was celebrated as the brave discoverer of America, rather than as a brutal colonizer.[50] Thanksgiving was a day of thanks, and the Pilgrims were heroes, not the oppressors of indigenous peoples.

Students were taught the framework of how the American government functioned with emphasis on the wisdom of the Founders and the importance of separation of powers.

According to Caldwell, major shifts in education began the Civil Rights movement of the 1960s which drove Progressives to re-imagine minorities as a fixed, and persistently oppressed group. The Civil Rights Acts of 1964 and 1968 mandated that corrective approaches be taken to the injustices of slavery and post-Reconstructionist Jim Crow laws (Caldwell, 2020). "Affirmative action" programs favoring "peoples of color" above "whites" for positions in the workplace and in universities were instituted. Preferential treatment was later extended to other historically "oppressed" groups, including women, the LGBTQ com-

---

48 The history of the Pledge of Allegiance is complicated. It was written in 1892 by the minister Francis Bellamy. In its original form it read, "I pledge allegiance to my Flag and the Republic for which it stands, one nation, indivisible, with liberty and justice for all." In 1923, it was amended to read, "I pledge allegiance to the Flag of the United States of America and to the Republic for which it stands, one nation, indivisible, with liberty and justice for all." In 1954, in response to a perceived Communist threat, President Eisenhower encouraged Congress to add the words "under God," creating the thirty-one-word pledge we say today. "I pledge allegiance to the flag of the United States of America, and to the republic for which it stands, one nation under God, indivisible, with liberty and justice for all." The reference to God has been repeatedly challenged by Progressive and atheist groups.

49 In 1978, The ACLU took an unpopular stance by defending the right of Nazis to parade in Skokie, Illinois. The current ACLU would seek to shut down even the mildest of politically incorrect positions today. It's come a long way.

50 Columbus was a brutal colonizer, as were virtually all of the Spanish explorers in the new World. But he did discover new continents, which surely must count for something. One rarely hears Progressives criticizing Spain for its approach to indigenous American natives, as the goal is to denigrate the United States.

munity, and the disabled.

This focus on the disenfranchised in society shifted educational emphasis away from the content of education to one of societal purpose. Currently, rather than emphasizing the centrality of the individual in a Lockean sense, a Progressive education focuses on tribalism based on *diversity, cultural identity,* and developing a *critical socially engaged intelligence* that will enable students to actively participate in the affairs of their community to achieve the "common good." Progressive educators have opposed separating academic education from vocational training, and have resisted attendance at charter schools, despite substantial evidence that children who attend them are academically more successful. (Sowell, 2011)

Open classrooms, schools without walls, cooperative learning, multiage approaches, social curriculum, and experiential education are all part of the current Progressive educational system that traces its roots to Dewey's ideas. Scholars, educators, and activists are currently exploring how to adopt Progressive ideas to questions, including global capitalism, cultural change, and planetary health. Simply put, the goal of Progressive education is no longer to teach facts and skills; rather, it is to sculpt an activist citizen who is primarily concerned with "social justice," as importantly, it retains Dewey's emphasis on a critical leadership role for elites as guides the future of society. This is the undergraduate education that most medical students born after 1960 would likely have received prior to attending university, where Progressive ideas would next be more incisively imparted.

HIGHER EDUCATION

According to US Census Bureau's data, nearly ninety-four million Americans ages twenty-five and over, i.e., 42 percent of the US population, hold associate, bachelor's, graduate, or professional degrees.

"Scholars" in the university are the source of much of the inspiration for Progressive ideas that are being espoused in the culture. These have incorporated critical theory, a key aspect of Marxist thought, originally formulated with the aim of undermining capitalist society. But in America, the major emphasis has not been on wealth discrepancies, as it was for Marx, as that would not serve the interests of the corporate elite who currently hold the lion's share of wealth. Instead, the alternative approach toward restructuring America has been to focus on its history of slavery and to stoke divisions based on race.

A recent product of this neo-Progressive approach is the *1619 Project,* conceived by "woke" Progressive journalists at the *New York Times*. The *1619 Project* reframes America's founding, and indeed all of American history, through the prism of slavery and race, seeking to propagate this perspective as standard curriculum throughout the educational system. But like much current Progressive neo-Marxist thought, it purposefully neglects and distorts history to achieve its aims. For example, it conveniently ignores the fact that at the time of America's founding virtually all societies were actively engaged in the slave trade. It was practiced in Africa and throughout the Islamic Ottoman Empire. Only in Western Europe, and after many centuries, had slavery grown unpopular. Most of the opposition to slavery took place in America, where a Civil War was fought in large measure to free slaves in the South (McLaughlin, 2022). None of this is considered in the *1619 Project*.

Numerous professional historians criticized the *Project* for its distorted factual claims. Its creators countered with the pointed argument that facts "don't matter," and that only the political ends achieved by reframing the Founding do. Certainly, this is not history as it has evolved as an academic discipline since the time of Herodotus; rather, it echoes the Progressive educational goal of raising students to become socially engaged activists. As Nikole Hannah-Jones wrote in a response to critics of the *Project:*

> I've always said that the *1619 Project* is not history. It is a work of journalism that explicitly seeks to challenge the national narrative and therefore, the national memory. The project has always been as much about the present as it is the past. (Rindsberg, 2021)

The current trend of judging America's history by today's moral standards necessarily distorts it. But this approach is currently condoned and transmitted by many American teachers to students at all grade levels. Those teachers who resist the change have been soundly criticized by politicians, local school boards, and the National Education Association. What matters to Progressives is adopting the educational system for the purpose of indoctrinating young minds into its agenda.

A major strategy of Progressive education has been to promote "political correctness." This is an insidious tactic that seeks to purge language of all references that might be perceived as psychologically injurious to others. It is antithetical to both classical Liberalism and Conservatism, as it denies the right guaranteed by the First Amendment to speak freely without fear of recriminations. But Progressives argue that the goal of eliminating discrimination is a higher moral calling than any guarantees of free speech. Determining what is "politically correct (PC)" speech has been a moving target, depending on what Progressives elites say it is at any given time.

Critical Race Theory (CRT), derived from Marxist ideology, is another part of the Progressive educational agenda. CRT frames members of society as either "oppressors" or "oppressed." In America, all "white men" have been assigned the role of "oppressors," and all peoples of color are "oppressed." This overtly racist classification has given rise to a cottage industry of educational "experts" who have enriched themselves in recent years by exposing "unconscious racial bias" and revealing "white fragility" in books and lectures at educational and corporate institutions, including corporate hospitals. Efforts at refuting the unsubstantiated claims of CRT have been met with stiff resistance from Progressive politicians, school boards, and the Teachers Union, with the claim that those who oppose CRT are *racists*. *Ad hominem* attacks have replaced civil discourse at all levels of society, as Progressives cynically use liberties guaranteed by the First Amendment to silence opposition. Dissenting Americans who fear the social consequences of being labeled as "racist" and who wish to avoid losing their jobs have chosen to remain quiet.

THE PROGRESSIVE CORPORATE HOSPITAL

For a host of ideological, legal, and economic reasons, corporations have aligned themselves with Progressive positions, a trend that began during the Presidency of Barack Obama. Indeed, my first glimpse into the Progressive transformation of the medical system occurred on the day of Obama's first inauguration in 2008. That morning, I received an e-mail message from my department head that all staff members were required to watch the televised inauguration in a prepared conference room. At the time, I recall thinking it both unusual and inappropriate to insist that anyone be required, or even asked, to celebrate the results of a political election at the workplace. Certainly, it had not happened previously.

When I first began practicing medicine in the 1970s, I had colleagues who held different political opinions. Some were liberal, as many were conservative. Indeed, medicine on the whole had been a politically conservative profession until the 1960s. Today pockets of conservatism persist in the medical profession but they rarely assume leadership positions in academic medical centers. This is because the corporate hospital is closely aligned with the political goals of Progressivism and now serves as part of its educational arm. Physicians are continuously exposed to progressive ideas and are expected to implement them into their practice.

But not all physicians share these views. Instead, a recent survey suggests that the political views of physicians tend to track with their practice specialty:

New data show that, in certain medical fields, large majorities of physicians tend to share the political leanings of their colleagues, and a study suggests ideology could affect some treatment recommendations. In surgery, anesthesiology, and urology, for example, around two-thirds of doctors who have registered a political affiliation are Republicans. In infectious disease, medicine, psychiatry, and pediatrics, more than two-thirds are Democrats. (Sanger-Katz, 2016)

This observation likely reflects underlying psychological predispositions that lead to choosing a medical specialty. Surgeons primarily work with concrete realities and have a reputation for being "doers" rather than "thinkers." To illustrate the point, a diseased gall bladder is reliably located in the right upper quadrant of the abdomen; the surgeon knows how to remove it and inspect it for evidence of pathology. Surgery is rooted in the concrete aspects of physicality. It requires a very different skill set than, e.g., the psychiatrist, whose role is to listen to and interpret the immaterial thoughts of others. In general, it is fair to say that most medical internists generally view themselves as more "cerebral" than their surgical colleagues.

But stereotypes can be misleading. There are many thoughtful surgeons, as well as interventionalist medical internists who perform minor surgeries. But as a rule, those who deal with concrete realities rather than abstractions are more likely to hold conservative views, and this is what the survey showed. Other differences likely play a role. For example, more women practice pediatrics (63 percent), psychiatry

(41 percent), and family medicine (38 percent) than general surgery, although most gynecological surgeons today are women. Voting patterns show that college-educated urban and suburban men and women tend to hold Progressive political views and will vote for Progressive Democratic candidates, as they did in the last Presidential election.

In the past, politics was rarely a topic of discussion at the workplace. But since the 1990s, the hospital atmosphere has grown increasingly political and hostile toward conservatives and their ideas. The imposition of Progressive mores on hospital workers intensified following Trump's election in 2016. Reservations about openly declaring the Progressive positions of the corporate hospital were swept aside, and the hospital leadership took the occasion to declare its political activism.[51] After all, Progressive education had primed them to act as socially concerned citizens, and now they felt called upon to rise to the occasion, as Trump's election challenged the Progressive agenda that they believed had somehow been "ordained" by Obama's election.

Admittedly, Trump was not "woke," and he had expressed little patience for the "political correctness" that Progressives were advocating. My colleagues expressed a distaste for Trump that spilled over to everything connected to him. Physicians at a neighboring Boston hospital went as far as to protest Melania Trump's visit to comfort sick children, somehow viewing that benign act of kindness as heinous. Yet, when I have questioned colleagues, few could cogently explain the intensity of their ill feeling.

When I openly acknowledged that I supported Trump, colleagues with whom I had been friends for decades stopped speaking to me. One morning, I entered my office to find a roll of toilet paper with Trump's face imprinted on each sheet. I tossed it into the wastebasket and did

---

51 Many today warn that if Trump were to be re-elected in 2024 that it would trigger the same response and lead to increased civil unrest. However, to imagine that the response to *any* conservative would be different is likely naïve.

not report the incident, as I knew that a complaint would not be greeted sympathetically by the hospital administration. All previous standards of fairness had broken down; only Progressive ideas were tolerated, and conservatives had no recourse.

When Trump placed a ban on immigration from countries where migrants could not be vetted, the dean of the medical school issued an e-mail to the staff denouncing his actions and declaring that they opposed medical school policies. More e-mails followed whenever Trump issued an executive order that opposed Progressive aims. For the first time in my years working at the hospital, I recognized that my political beliefs were in violation of "policy."

At the same time, the hospital's "HR and Diversity" bureaucracy was flourishing, with new HR offices proliferating on the hospital campus. Signs on bathrooms now advertised them as "Unisex." Tables in hospital administrative offices were littered with pamphlets lauding LGTBQ rights. Gender-sensitive pronouns were introduced into medical practice. Currently, all busy professional staff is compelled by hospital administrations to complete hours of CRT-inspired modules. Those who reject the accusation of racism are taught that this is due to unconscious or subliminal racism. The hospital was all in with the Progressive political agenda. But it was not—and still is not— clear to me why a hospital, whose primary goal should be to treat disease, would choose not to remain neutral on these topics. A fundamental shift had occurred; the Progressive notion of social activism was now dominant.

But I found the behavior of some of my colleagues to be curious. I knew from past conversations that some of the older ones had in the past held staunch conservative views, whereas most of the younger staff were clearly Progressives. As Caldwell suggested, when they were educated had been an important factor in how they positioned themselves in the culture wars. In addition, it was long recognized that tend to grow more conservative with age, so differences based on age came as no surprise.[52] But why would my once conservative older colleagues now claim to be Progressives? Virtually none of them could discuss the philosophical merits of Progressivism versus Conservatism or were social activists. What happened?

THE EXPECTATIONS OF OTHERS

It is a reasonably straightforward task to discuss the influences of politics and money on the medical profession, as one can present published papers and statistics on these topics to assist in formulating an argument; it is more difficult to discuss what might motivate behavior, as motives are generally hidden from view. An approach to this topic often requires the insight of a trained psychologist, and as Freud noted, all behavior is multidetermined, so no single explanation will suffice in characterizing it. What follows is a discussion of the psychology of physicians today, but it might well apply to other professionals in elite society as well. I have spent hours pondering what is transpiring in my profession based on my interactions, and what follows in this section is my attempt to make sense of my observations. The necessary disclaimer to what follows is that it takes a broad brush to an entire profession and that it will not necessarily apply to all. Nevertheless, what follows does capture important truths that will allow insight into what is transpiring in medicine today.

One may begin with the fact that man is a social animal, and his

---

52 The saying that , "If you are not a liberal when young, you have no heart, and if not conservative when old you have no mind," is often attributed to Winston Churchill. But he was not the first to make the statement. Rather the full quote originated with a nineteenth century jurist, Anselmne Batbie, and is as follows: "He who is not a républican at twenty compels one to doubt the generosity of his heart; but he who, after thirty, persists, compels one to doubt the soundness of his mind."

interactions are driven by conflicting desires to affiliate versus remaining separate from others. All human societies tend to develop hierarchies of power. Indeed, studies of the behavior of chimpanzees, our closest primate relatives, have demonstrated that struggles to achieve dominance occur regularly. (C. Ferguson, 2021)

For this reason, perhaps the simplest explanation of what is transpiring in the culture today is that it represents a struggle between powerful elites who dominate the institutions of the culture and those who are have less influence. Progressives over the years have strategically positioned themselves to control the major institutions within the culture, including local and federal government, the educational system, the arts, and the media. Their power in this regard has been consolidated, and they behave as though they are now unassailable. Unfortunately, as Lord Acton noted, "Power tends to corrupt, and absolute power corrupts absolutely. Great men are almost always bad men, even when they exercise influence and not authority, still more when you superadd the tendency or the certainty of corruption by authority." So it is little surprise that as power has been secured, the corruption of Progressive institutions has ensued.

Physicians can be numbered amongst the elites in society, and consequently tend to be aligned with Progressive positions on a host of matters. But how do intelligent people bring themselves to believe in the correctness of some of the extreme positions adopted in recent years by Progressives? Can physicians not object to the irrational aspects of the current Progressive agenda?

What has changed in the culture of medicine may not be its new heartfelt concern for social justice; rather, it is as likely a need to meet the expectations of others. There is a story in the *Talmud* (*Berachot* 28b) in which the first-century sage, Rabban Yochanan ben Zakkai, is on his death bed surrounded by students. They beseech him for a last blessing. He responds, "May it be His will that the fear of heaven be upon you like the fear of flesh and blood." The students are stunned. Surely, they argue, a respectable blessing would be for the fear of heaven to surpass the fear of human beings? "Ah, would that it were that way," answers the Rabbi. "For when a person sins, he says 'Let no man see.' Would that we cared as much about what God thinks as about what people think." Ben Zakkai's insight is applicable today, two thousand years later.

As *Facebook* executives realized, the social pressures to be accepted and approved of are arguably the strongest motivators of human behavior. Few will summon the courage to stand apart from the prevailing opinions of the crowd. Instead, people tend to lose their cognitive and emotional autonomy in a group. As Jung noted:

> A group experience takes place on a lower level of consciousness than the experience of an individual. This is due to the fact that, when many people gather together to share one common emotion, the total psyche emerging from the group is below the level of the individual psyche. (Jung, 1962)

The individual in a group may behave in uncharacteristic ways. Jung noted that some become "cocky," confident that they will be supported if they behave in ways that they would not on their own. This explains much of the vile behavior seen on social media, where scathing statements are posted by otherwise reserved individuals.[53] On their own, I am confident that none of my colleagues would be capable of the prank of leaving a roll of toilet paper on a colleague's desk, but with the support of a group, someone apparently felt safe enough to do just that.

Groups with strongly held ideological beliefs tend to scapegoat others. Psychologically speaking, scapegoating is a projective defense, in

---

53 The Holiness Code (Exodus 20) of the Hebrew bible warns "You must not follow the crowd in doing wrong." 3:2

which the disavowed feelings and actions of an *in-group* are misattributed to an *out-group*. But it must be emphasized that projection is not a fully conscious phenomenon. Indeed, Jung warned that the greatest threat facing modern society was the propensity to project unconscious hostilities onto others. In such states of unawareness, it is possible to justify perpetrating harm on others. Projections of hostility are currently being used to silence opposition (*shadow banning, removal from social media*), persecute others (*cancel culture, dismissal from jobs*), and in the extreme, removing them physically from society (*concentration camps for the unvaccinated, imprisonment of peaceful January 6 Capitol protestors*). Certainly, some accusations have come from ruthless politicians who will say virtually anything to maintain themselves in power. But for many, it reflects unconsciousness of motive, and that it is so widespread is disturbing.[54]

Excessive projective defenses are characteristic of paranoid psychopathology. They emerge in individuals with rigid character, perfectionism, an inability to confront uncomfortable ideas and feelings, and suspicious tendencies. The intensity of projection in societal discourse is greater today than I have witnessed in my lifetime. The implications of this should be of concern to all, as it suggests that many Americans may be slipping into states of mental illness. Paranoid ideation can be accompanied by overt displays of hostility and destructiveness.

Unfortunately, it is virtually impossible to convince the paranoid that his thinking processes are skewed. He is suspicious and holds fixed ideas that cannot be reasoned with. The paranoid feels compelled to monitor everything around him and make efforts to control them, out

---

54 There is perhaps no clearer or serious example of a projection than the accusations that constituted the Russia hoax in which Trump was accused of colluding with Russia to defeat Hillary Clinton. It has proven to be the case, despite numerous denials, that the Clinton campaign had conspired with the help of operatives to smear the Trump campaign and the story is still unfolding. But virtually all of the accusations against Trump proved to be projections of what Democrats were doing themselves.

of fear of himself losing control and being harmed. But this is always a projection of his own hostility. So, it is easy to appreciate why paranoid Progressive leaders in Washington might imagine that all conservative protesters were trying to kill them on January 6, or as Alexandria Ocasio Cortes suggested, "rape" her.[55] Those who seek "safe spaces" for fear of being harmed by words or COVID-19 may also qualify as paranoid in many instances.

The notion that anyone who takes issue with the Progressive agenda is a "white supremacist" or a "Nazi" is not consistent with reality. Yet, many Progressives today sincerely believe this, and because they are insulated in their own groups, they are free to do so unchallenged. When peaceful protesting truckers in the US and Canada are labeled "insurrectionists," while "Black Lives Matter" and "Antifa" rioters are judged as peaceful, it is not simply blatant hypocrisy as conservatives often will label it, but more likely the expression of a shared delusion, and that should trouble all of us, as it implies that many in society are currently mentally unstable and/or have been brainwashed by propaganda.

When groups hold strong ideological beliefs, individual responsibility and accountability may be denied. Whereas most conservatives espouse the values of Enlightenment liberalism, with its emphasis on freedom of speech, the rights of the individual, and private property, according to the current Progressive/Marxist cultural narrative, the *group,* not the individual, is most valued. As a consequence, conservative arguments that support the rights of the individual fall on deaf ears, as the Progressive/Marxist preferred mode of governance is authoritarian or totalitarian.

As the philosopher, Roger Scruton writes in *Conservatism,*

---

55 Unfortunately, paranoia is virtually a staple of those who enter politics. Most manage to keep it to some degree under wraps, but we are currently seeing a great outpouring of paranoid ideation and behaviors from Progressives in government.

It is precisely the character of modern utopias to ignore limits—to imagine societies without law (Marx and Engels), without families (Laing), without borders or defenses (Sartre). And much conservative ink has been wasted (me among others) in rebutting such views, which can be believed only by people who are *unable to perceive realities, and who therefore will never be persuaded by argument.* (Scruton, 2017) (Present author's italics)

Scruton's point is well-taken. The current avatar of Progressivism can more properly be termed "liberal fundamentalism," as its devotees hold the equivalent of apocalyptic religious beliefs, including radical dualistic notions of "good versus evil," that are not open to civil disagreements (R. Kradin, 2018). The current avatar of Progressivism is more properly termed "liberal fundamentalism." As a large percentage of Americans today can no longer be reasoned with, it will not be possible to construct a cooperative society with them in the future, absent significant change.

But rigid cultural narratives of *any* type have no place in the practice of medicine, which must be maintained separately from them. Unfortunately, the corporate hospital has placed politics, money, and power ahead of its proper mission, which is simply to care for the sick. It has instead ignored, distorted, and denied objective truths that conflict with an ideological mission.

KNOW THY ROLE

In his model of the personality, Jung discussed the importance of the *persona*. He defined it as the part of the personality that engages with the outside world, determined, in part, by the expectations of others. Simply, it is the role that one is expected to play in society.[56] A limited set of behaviors is expected from the archetypal role of *The*

---

56 Persona is the Greek word for mask. These masks were used in ancient Greek theater to define the role of the actor.

Physician. He is expected to be knowledgeable in the art and science of medicine, and to hold the best interests of his patients foremost in mind. No other calling should be allowed to interfere with these goals when a physician is in role.

The same can be said of the sick individual while in the role of *The Patient.* His only goal is should be to cooperate with the physician in an effort to become well. What the *individual* physician or patient does when out of role is their business and no one else's concern. Indeed, the *persona* should be cast off when the individual is not in role, lest it becomes a permanent rigid facade. The physician who allows political, economic, and cultural biases to distort his *persona*, denies his proper role in society.[57] [58] And this is the current source of conflict for physicians. Progressive education suggests that it is everybody's proper role to act as an activist in society. What we have learned from the pandemic is that being a physician can be incompatible with political activism and physicians who fail to recognize this endanger their patients and do damage to their profession.

Unfortunately, Progressive cultural narratives have deeply infiltrated the medical practice, and they have tainted it. This accounts for positions being espoused by America's major medical agencies. The American Medical Association (AMA), once a conservative voice in the culture, has embraced Progressive "wokeness," to the detriment of patients, as the following article in the *Washington Examiner* suggests:

> Suppose you were hoping that your doctor's office would remain one of the few remaining places free of the politically correct

---

57 This point is not limited to physicians. It appears that many in society have lost track of what their roles properly are. The mantra of activism extends to all fields. Teachers no longer teach; students no longer learn. All are moved as James Joyce said by "pornography," i.e., by factors beyond the essence of their true purpose.

58 This important lesson constitutes the climactic theme of the Hindu Bhagavad Gita, in which the hero Arjuna is conflicted about going to war with members of his extended family. He is warned by the god Krishna that it is his dharma, i.e., his role in society to act as a warrior.

police. In that case, we have some bad news for you: The *American Medical Association* has gone "woke."

In conjunction with the Association of American Medical Colleges Center for Health Justice, the AMA recently released a document titled *Advancing Health Equity: A Guide to Language, Narrative, and Concepts.*

The "toolkit" is designed to help physicians and health-care workers achieve "health equity," which strives to correct gaps in health outcomes that are "unjust, avoidable, unnecessary, and unfair."

The elimination of personal responsibility and accountability are critical to this "health equity" effort. "Inequities cannot be understood or adequately addressed if we focus only on individuals, their behavior, or their biology," the guide reads. Instead, "health equity work requires" the identification and disruption of "dominant narratives" that "limit our understanding of the root causes of health inequities."

"Narratives grounded in white supremacy and sustaining structural racism, for example, perpetuate cumulative disadvantage for some populations and cumulative advantage for white people, especially white men," the guide explains. "Narratives that uncritically center meritocracy and individualism render invisible the genuine constraints generated and reinforced by poverty, discrimination, and ultimately exclusion."

Turning to how doctors should disrupt dominant narratives when talking to patients, the guide laments "the overwhelming focus on changing individual behavior to improve health, mostly avoiding the social and economic conditions which generate poor health outcomes." Instead, when some patients fail to follow through with a health plan advised by their doctor, which the guide identifies as a dominant "non-compliance" narrative, doctors should instead consider "the significant barriers faced by the patients in their lives, from not having enough money to pay for their medications, or not having the capability to take time off work, or not being able to secure affordable childcare to participate in an activity."

So, the next time you see the doctor and he starts to harangue you about exercising more and eating well, be sure to point out you would have exercised more and eaten more veggies, but the big, evil corporations are just making it too hard.

Unless you are a white male, of course, in which case everything wrong in the world is your fault, and you probably deserve to be sick anyway. (Carroll, 2021)

The problem with scientific institutions promoting Progressive ideas is that the positions that they adopt often lack scientific credibility. Take again, for example, "equity," an abstract concept that is unscientific because it never occurs normally as a part of human nature. Physicians who argue for equity engage in "doublethink," as freedom of *choice*, a liberty that they concomitantly espouse, and "equity" cannot co-exist. What Marx failed to appreciate in his musings on economic class conflict is that human nature ultimately abhors "equity." It flies in the face of Darwinian competition and leaves those who embrace it diminished and demotivated. Consequently, "equity" can only be forcefully *imposed* on others, via authoritarianism, totalitarianism, or fascism. Indeed, Ferguson argues that the socioeconomic success of English North America over Spanish South America was largely due to the North's allowance for social mobility based on hard work and merit, whereas South America was founded on a rigid caste system in which the underclass was never able to rise. (Ferguson, 2011)

Furthermore, for physicians to argue in favor of "equity" is frankly ludicrous. Physicians are amongst the most accomplished privileged members of American society. In the vast majority of cases, their careers were established based on merit, and few would seriously consider applying the idea of "equity" to themselves or their family. They are either disingenuous and/or in the throes of a self-defeating impulse. But interestingly, they do not appear to be suffering from cognitive dissonance as a result, likely because they have resolved this conflict through denial and projection. What can be said is that physicians who promote such Progressive ideas have not spent sufficient time in introspection pondering their ideological positions. But as part of a group, they do not have to.

AN INSULAR MEDICAL ELITE

Social scientists have noted how difficult it is for the observers of a sports event not to choose a side to root for, and suggest that there may be biological reasons for this:

> Although people report many reasons for following a favorite team, social connectedness is among the most frequently cited ...When we look at motivation for following a sport team, group affiliation is one of the top ones, and identifying strongly with a salient local team where other fans are in the environment—that's a benefit to social-psychological well-being.

> In a series of studies ...the results have been correlational but consistent: Higher identification with a team is associated with significantly lower levels of alienation, loneliness, and higher levels of collective self-esteem and positive emotion. (Wang, 2006)

While not all physicians are ardent sports fans, some unquestionably see themselves as part of a "team." My medical career was unusual, as I practiced as part of three different hospital departments and tended to see areas of potential cooperation between them. But I soon discovered that there was little interest in cooperation, as each department "team" was primarily interested in how they could benefit to the exclusion of the other.

Insularity fosters perspectival homogeneity. In *Coming Apart*, social critic Charles Murray argues that America's elites are diverging from the rest of society, and he views insularity as a large part of the present cultural problem (Murray, 2012). The majority of the physicians hail from elite backgrounds and were born into professional and "medical" families. They attended Progressive private schools and universities together. According to a recent article that details a court case against Harvard University for unfair admission practices against Asian students, private school education constitutes a wedge issue in society :

> There's a clear tell in this strategy that reveals Students for Fair Admissions (SFFA) does not really care about unearned advantages: It said nothing about graduating from a private high school. Graduating from private high school is a far larger advantage at many top-ranked colleges than playing sports or being a legacy or even having a connection to a donor are. (Viewed a certain way, a private school is almost a more reliable income source for an elite college than a donor.) While 10 percent of students admitted to Harvard Class of 2018 were recruited athletes and 12 percent were legacies, almost 40 percent of the class went to private school. If we really wanted to get rid of the most glaring case of bias at prestigious private universities, we would target private high school students.(Murphy, 2021)

As a consequence of their insular background, it is virtually assured that they will also seek information from Progressive news sources, which today may lead them to be grossly misinformed about what is really transpiring in the world around them. In this regard, my story is worth recounting.

Like many of my physician colleagues, I was a *CNN* viewer and had considered it a reliable news source. Although like most of the media it was known to have a liberal bias, until recently, CNN news would have been considered "mainstream." But my opinion concerning this changed during the 2016 Presidential campaign. At that time, the networks allotted considerable time to covering Donald Trump's campaign speeches. Its viewers were curious about his flamboyant style, and Trump increased their viewer market share. But the post-speech commentary on CNN and the other mainstream media channels was consistently critical and did not concord with what I had seen and heard. Points made by Trump were invariably misrepresented and made to sound dangerous, to a degree that I decided to explore how he was being covered by other channels.

Fox News has for years been portrayed by the Progressive elite as a news station that caters to the "Far-Right" and to the "uneducated." I rarely watched it and knew few who did. But when I began to view *Fox's* coverage of Trump's speeches, it was clear to me that it was factually more accurate than CNN's. When I tried to convey this to my colleagues, they dismissed it as "nonsense" and were unwilling to consider a different perspective. When after the election, I attempted to point out many of the positive accomplishments of the Trump administration, they had not heard of them and didn't believe them. One day, a young female asked me one day how I could support Trump, as he was putting illegal immigrant children into "cages" at the border. I attempted to explain that these were the same facilities that Obama had built during his administration and that it was standard procedure to separate children from adults following an arrest, and that families would be reunited. I didn't bother trying to explain that illegal immigration was a crime. She had never heard that side of the story before, and I don't think that she believed it.

The Progressive elite denies that corporate media networks, including CNN, MSNBC, CBS, NBC, etc., as well as major social media networks, are peddling propaganda, and no amount of information will change their opinion, although viewership has fallen precipitously since Trump left the White House. News outlets help to create audience bubbles, where truths can be distorted, suppressed, and fabricated—and people libeled—all in the service of preserving an ideological narrative. Errors in reporting are not followed by retractions, apologies, or consequences.

Arguably, the most grievous travesties occurred in the lead-up to the 2020 Presidential campaign, when facts that would have been critical for an informed electorate to hear were suppressed by Progressive news sources, in order to guarantee Trump's defeat. These included hiding Joe Biden's obvious cognitive difficulties from public view, spreading false information concerning the coronavirus pandemic, denying that violent riots were taking place in America's major cities during the summer of 2020, and discounting compelling evidence of corruption by the Biden family. As the *Washington Times* journalist Mollie Hemingway has suggested in *Rigged*, to doubt that the 2020 election was manipulated is to deny reality. (Hemingway, 2021)

Propaganda is the falsification of facts to fit a cultural and political narrative, and unfortunately, most of America's major news networks are currently broadcasting propaganda:

> In contemporary society, propaganda has a major impact due to the new technologies in the media (satellite television, the Internet) that ensure the rapid and instant transmission of information, thus expanding the audience. The concept of propaganda acts systematically in support of a doctrine, in order to persuade a large mass of individuals. It is generally associated with a negative action, considered to be reprehensible, and this is the consequence of the attempts that various totalitarian regimes have manifested abusively. Basically, propaganda is a conscious communication act with a political and revolutionary character representing a strategy of social influence. The element of difference is misinformation. Thus, this concept can be one of integration and consolidation of the society or, on the contrary, it can be a factor of agitation. (Rusu & Herman, 2018)

But these lies are never admitted; instead, the conservative news outlets have been accused of spreading "misinformation," which represents another projection. Trump's accusation that the American press has been acting as an "enemy of the people" is not exaggerated.

The screenwriter, Paddy Chayefsky, presciently predicted the behavior of today's corporate news media networks in his 1976 film *Network*. In it, he portrayed the decline of professional journalism, as it was being replaced by entertainment and propaganda in order to increase corporate profits. Chayefsky foresaw that when corporate monopolies controlled the news, they would use it to persuade the viewing public to accept a globalist economic vision of the future rather than to tell the truth. And that is what is happening in 2022.

COMPLIANCE AND PERFECTIONISM

Propaganda is only effective if an audience accepts it. I was taught by a psychiatry professor that medical students are the *ideal* subjects on which to conduct psychological experiments because, as a group, they are exceedingly compliant and have been conditioned to accept authority. We've all seen actors playing physicians on TV, making tough decisions that buck the hospital establishment. In my youth, it was *Ben Casey* and *Dr. Kildare*. More recently it's been *ER*, *Gray's Anatomy, and House*. But this characterization is far from the truth. While there are idealistic young physicians who choose to confront injustice, they are the exception to the rule.

The reason is not difficult to comprehend, considering what it takes to become a physician in the twenty-first century. In order to gain admission to medical school, you must have a stellar academic record, as well as other accomplishments that set you apart from the pack. There is *no* room for error. Many medical school applicants today will have a 4.0 grade-point average (straight A's), near-perfect scores on their qualifying entrance tests, and will have spent time working in Africa or on an Indian (Native-American) reservation. The *ultra-accomplished* will have started a biotech company and have several patents under their belt, and the majority of first-year medical students are only twenty-two years of age.

What inspires one to become such an *uber*-overachiever? Is it out of love for the projects one has embarked upon? Undoubtedly, for some it is; but that may not be the most common reason. As a group, physicians are extremely goal-oriented and hardworking. I had a colleague whose life's goal was to be a Harvard Professor of Medicine. He worked feverishly at it, conducting research, writing papers, attending meetings, and networking with colleagues. But when he received his promotion, he closed his lab, stopped writing papers, and no longer attended meetings. He had achieved what he wanted and no longer needed to perform.

There are several pathways toward achieving success in academic medicine. One is to be substantially more talented than the rest of your colleagues and to earn a place based on an outstanding achievement. As one might imagine, that is not the most common path. Instead, most will succeed by working *very* hard and taking little time out for play.[59] A third option, rarely openly discussed, is to come from an influential, wealthy, "legacy" family that has contributed generations to the medical profession. This is common in the Ivy League, and one recognizes the family names. Finally, you can be a member of an identity group that is currently viewed as "oppressed," and succeed via affirmative action, with less than stellar credentials.[60]

---

59 An emphasis on joyless hard work characterizes the obsessive-compulsive personality. I had several colleagues who claimed that they had never taken a vacation and would never unless they could rationalize it as part of a work situation, e.g., giving an invited lecture.

60 Despite what those who champion affirmative action say, studies show that this path often leads to failure. A mediocre student *of any color*, when placed in a class of highly intelligent overachievers, will tend to do poorly, whereas the same student might have a better chance of success at and academically lower ranked medical school. But rather than admit that, schools would prefer to do away with grading systems, so as not to compromise their belief in *equity*.

GETTING TO THE TOP

The drive to become a physician rarely emerges spontaneously. In most cases, it is strategically inserted into a young mind by an ambitious parent. There are the standard jokes about the Asian tiger mother who each time she passes her child's nursery inquires, "Are you doctor yet?" or of the Jewish mother who introduces her toddler as, "Meet my son the doctor." Alternatively, some may be inspired by early personal or family members with illness.

I consider myself lucky to have had parents who displayed little interest in my career path. For a variety of reasons, it was not on their radar screen. They knew that I was a good student and assumed that I would find an area of work that interested me and that my life would work out, and they were right. This allowed me a far greater degree of freedom than many of my classmates. One young friend of mine was hardly ever allowed out of his house because, as his mother informed me daily, "Eugene has to study." At the time, I felt sorry for him, and for myself, as this parental stance complicated my ability to find someone to play with. Parenthetically, Eugene never met his parents' high expectations despite all his studying, and eventually settled on a career selling retail. Hopefully, he is happy and occasionally has time to play.

Some of my fellow students would rebel as teenagers against the pressure placed upon them by narcissistic parents. This mode of sabotage can be successful if a young person then manages to find his own path. But for others, it can herald the beginning of a life of repetitive failures. Those who continue on the path set for them may eventually be rewarded for their compliance and hard work. However, years of an oppressive upbringing can lead to substantial unmetabolized anger, although the compliant person generally learns to guise it. Consequently, many physicians can be annoyingly passive-aggressive.

And it doesn't matter whether they are highly successful or not; their anger somehow manages to find a mode of expression. Dr. Fauci is a good example of a passive-aggressive physician. If you observe him with this in mind, you will recognize the tell-tale signs of his effect on others. His answers to questions will obfuscate and frustrate; he will smoothly undermine colleagues and political higher-ups, and do it all with a twisted smile. Unfortunately, America is now paying the price for his neuroticism.

At university, basic science courses are crowded with hopeful pre-medical students. Due to the pressure to succeed, they tend to be anxious, envious, secretive, and even paranoid. It is common for them to maneuver to attend classes that are not too difficult, and to seek out professors with reputations for being "easy graders." Beyond that, few express much interest in the subject matter that they are studying. Education is merely a stepping stone toward achieving a goal.

Some thirty years after graduating from medical school, I had the opportunity to study for a post-graduate certificate in a field that had interested me for years and that I had not previously had the time for. I was in a large class with other physicians, some of whom had been practicing for years and who needed the course certificate for sundry purposes. I was surprised to see that their behaviors had not changed a bit from their pre-medical training. Prior to the final examination, fifty-somethings could still be seen frantically searching for copies of old tests, and engaging in planned study/strategy sessions with the younger students. When I finally asked one why he was so concerned, since virtually no one failed the course and the grade would neither add nor detract from his career, he was perplexed by the question. This was simply the way that it's done. He worried daily that he would not pass the test, only to receive the highest grade in the class. Many physicians are constantly worried for neurotic reasons to be discussed.

When I attended university, I had a chemistry professor who taught a compulsory pre-medical course attended by more than 100 students. He was an odd-looking man and known as a tough grader, and because of this, he was disliked by the pre-med students.

I had expressed a genuine interest in his area of research and, in turn, he took an interest in me. He researched the behavior of flames, which I thought was rather unusual and I was curious about it. It had *no* relevance to medicine, and consequently, was of no interest to most of the pre-medical students who were too busy worrying about their grade to be genuinely interested in anything.

At one point, he took me aside and in a fatherly manner asked me why I wanted to be a physician. He confided that he found most of the pre-medical students each year to be a rather unlikeable group and questioned whether I would be happy working among them for a lifetime. At the time, I listened, but apparently not well enough, as I thought that I would be able to navigate my own path toward happiness. But his concern was prophetic, as I spent my long medical career never particularly enjoying the company of most of my colleagues. Undoubtedly had I enjoyed them more, the tone of the present book might be different.

When I had the opportunity, years later, to teach medical students, like my old professor, I discovered that few were there genuinely to learn. I recall gazing out on an amphitheater of medical students, only to see a sea of incurious faces. Some were reading the newspaper; others had headphones on and were listening to God knows what. When I encountered this situation, I assumed that my teaching style was boring and needed improvement, but I was told by my colleagues that this was a universal experience.

THE PSYCHOLOGY OF THE MEDICAL ELITE

The history of medicine teaches that the reverence with which doctors are held in modern times is new. In days when effective treatments were few and far between, avoiding the doctor was probably a good idea. Certainly, there are numerous examples in history of physicians doing more harm than good.[61] Thankfully, today physicians are on firmer footing than in the past. Consequently, they can also be egotistic and imagine that they are the primary source of healing. It is easy to imagine that one has been responsible for healing a sick person, without appreciating that the vast majority of the healing process occurs spontaneously. The orthopedic surgeon who treats a broken bone will approximate the ends of the fracture, splint it, and then watch as the body does the rest. The vast amount of medical practice falls into this paradigm but few physicians actually ponder it. But as my old family physician once said, "God heals; doctors collect the fee."[62]

In the past, most physicians chose their careers out of interest. After all, it was hard work and not necessarily financially rewarding. A septuagenarian like myself can remember the haggard-looking fellow who came to the house when someone was ill at all hours carrying his black bag. Try to get a doctor to make a house-call today under any circumstance; it won't happen. You can have a fever of 106°F and expect to wait for an hour or more in the waiting room of a busy emergency room before being seen. After all, doctors are busy. But weren't they busy in the past? The answer is they were *busier*. But the old country doctor lacked something that today's physician has, and that is entitlement. In

---

61 There are many examples, but one that comes to mind is the final illness of George Washington. Washington contracted a tonsillar abscess (quinsy) in 1799. The doctors in attendance applied the modern medical technologies of the time, which was the application of leeches. Washington was subsequently bled multiple times and died shortly thereafter.

62 If you are an atheist, this can be rephrased to state that the vast majority of healing processes are innate and most medicines simply help move them along in the right direction.

the past, young people were not coddled and spoiled to the degree that many are today. It was difficult to get by with an entitled attitude in America. But that is no longer the case.

PHYSICIAN AS PETER PAN

It has been noted that the currently popular overprotective style of parenting has had an inhibitory effect on the maturation process of children (Lukianoff & Haidt, 2015). As a consequence of insular upbringing, many physicians never fully mature psychologically. This may be especially true for those who work in academic hospitals, as the hospital provides a safe place to practice and a reliable salary, so that one does not have to confront the challenges of private practice. When I attended my twenty-fifth medical school class reunion, I was astonished to find that those who had worked in private practice appeared on average some 10–20 years older than those who had worked in academic medicine. It sounds extraordinary, but it was as though the aging process for those in academics had actually slowed. And it was a total mind-body phenomenon, as many academic physician colleagues also retained a child-like naivete concerning the world around them, in some cases well into their dotage. Jung noted this phenomenon and referred to such characters as *puer aeturnus* (or *puella aeterna* in women), from the Latin for "eternal youth." Like *Peter Pan*, the *puer* refuses to age, and that fact is somehow reflected in both their psychology and physiology.

PROJECTION AND DENIAL

As a group, physicians can prove to be quite defensive when criticized. One of the unspoken cardinal rules of the hospital is not to criticize one's colleagues, likely because most physicians are already harsh on themselves, having incorporated a constant stream of critical voices in growing up. The prominent ego-defenses of physicians are projection and denial. The first allows them to blame others for their mistakes; the other allows them to refuse to acknowledge mistakes. One sees these operating in Dr. Fauci, as he defends against accusations from Congressmen for his pandemic performance. He refuses to accept either responsibility or accountability. But most physicians I have known will entertain substantial doubts concerning their competence and self-worth.

> I worked once with a young obsessional female resident who was highly perfectionistic and anxious about making a mistake. Her discomfort was palpable and frankly painful to watch. Out of compassion, I tried to soothe her by suggesting that although we try not to make mistakes, we all do. She broke down in tears and thanked me, claiming that she had never heard that before.

Unfortunately, my reassurance had little effect on her anxiety, as it is virtually impossible to reassure a perfectionist that mistakes are acceptable. And in truth, there is little room for error when caring for others, as mistakes can have serious consequences, making it difficult to condone fallibility.

Perfectionism leads to a host of problems and one has been to make effective teaching impossible. The Socratic method of asking probing questions no longer works with students today. When I was a medical resident in the 1970s, my fellow residents and I were eager to be asked challenging questions. It was seen as an opportunity to prove one's ability. It was a competitive and exciting atmosphere, and all appeared to have benefitted from it. But values and sensitivities have changed. Today, one encounters only sullen silence from students when they are asked questions. They resent being "put on the line" in the presence of others, as an incorrect answer would imply that there is something they don't know, and that would compromise their illusion of perfection.

Asking probing questions is now considered "mean."

As a result, teaching to any depth is not possible, even in one-on-one situations. Rather than admit that they might be ignorant on a topic, students will instead convey the impression that they already know what one is attempting to teach them. Consequently, it is not possible to assess accurately what they do and don't know.

Whereas evoking intellectual discomfort is a sin, the *cardinal* sin is any display of upset. During my training, I encountered a situation that poignantly illustrates that point.

> One night while working in the hospital emergency room, a young man entered with a drug overdose. He was unconscious and had labored breathing. The anesthesiologist's attempt to pass a breathing tube was unsuccessful, and a tracheostomy was required. The medical resident charged with the task suffered a sort of mental breakdown under the stress of the moment. He grabbed the nearest sharp instrument and proceeded to cut the man's neck, nearly all through, cursing uncontrollably, as this transpired. The young man died.
>
> The next day, the resident was summoned to meet with the Director of the Hospital, a distinguished silver-haired man who sported the Ivy League bow-tie and tweed jacket. He chided the resident, not for the horrendous medical performance that left a patient dead, rather for the "sin" of having lost his temper and cursed in front of the nurses.

If I had any doubts about the values of the hospital, they were dispelled on that day.

THE OBSESSIONAL ELITE

Everything that I have described until now can be attributed to rigid character. From a psychiatric perspective, it is fair to say that a large percentage of Progressive physicians meet the criteria for a diagnosis of obsessive-compulsive personality (OCP) (R. Kradin, 2018).

Diagnostically, OCP is characterized by rigid character, perfectionism, problems with self-direction, restricted affect, diminished empathy, a penchant for hard work, problems with achieving intimacy, and a compulsive need to control both themselves and those around them. It is diagnostically on a spectrum with narcissism and paranoid personality with overlaps being common. One might question whether these are the characteristics that people are ideally looking for in their physician. Nevertheless, based on the current criteria for admission, it is what medical schools are selecting for and consequently enriching the physician pool with.

Many physicians will proudly admit to having "OCD," [63] but they see it primarily as an attribute that leads them to do work hard and do a good job. They are right, as many high-functioning elite professionals meet the criteria for obsessionality. But they are rarely aware of the negative implications of their neurosis until later in life, when they experience problems with their marriage and other interpersonal relationships. There was an anecdote about one of the more "dedicated" physicians at the hospital that I worked at. It was said that his family never saw him and only knew that he had been home when they found "the toilet seat had been left up."

Physicians with OCP must learn to guise their restricted affect and lack of empathy in treating patients, but as the psychoanalyst David Shapiro notes, their "concern" for others does not represent genuine feeling:

> What makes the conscientiousness of the compulsive person special is different from the nature or the strength of his values, standards, or purposes ... When the compulsive person reminds himself

---

63 In the current diagnostic nomenclature, obsessive-compulsive disorder (OCD) refers to a crippling disorder characterized by unwanted intrusive thoughts and compulsive rituals. How exactly it relates to OCP is uncertain, but people with OCP are generally high-functioning. The term "OCD" has entered common parlance and anyone with a penchant for order and control may mistakenly refer to themselves as having "OCD."

that he should do something because it is the right thing, the nice thing, or the generous thing, he is prompted not by kindness, generosity, or concern for justice but by a sense of rules and duties to do something kind, generous, or nice (Shapiro, *Autonomy*, p. 80).

Indeed, this same behavior is seen in the "woke" personality. During the current pandemic, "woke" physicians wore their masks, indoors and out, and made certain that their children did as well, despite knowing that there was no data to support these behaviors. They socially distanced appropriately and received as many vaccinations as Dr. Fauci and the CDC suggested, again with little supporting evidence. In addition, they championed political correctness, critical race theory, etc.

It is difficult to understand why physicians would prioritize such ideological beliefs above their primary role as healers. Some may hold these beliefs to represent a "higher calling." In his musings on religion, Freud noted similarities between obsessive-compulsive rituals and the rituals of organized religion (Freud, 1907). This is not by chance, as they are rooted in the same archetypal core. As previously noted, "woke" Progressivism qualifies as a secular religion, but rather than worshipping God, it is primarily organized around the anxieties and morality of obsessional neurosis.

ESCAPE FROM FREEDOM

I was recently asked by an acquaintance why most intelligent physicians have not spoken out against the current handling of the pandemic. My answer was that, in part, it is because they have been taught to obey authority. Perhaps the most disturbing trend amongst Progressive physicians has been their willingness to divest themselves of freedom and to embrace authoritarianism. In *Escape from Freedom*, the social psychologist Erich Fromm examined what he referred to as the "authoritarian personality." Although Fromm does not equate this with the "obsessive-compulsive personality," their features are virtually identical.

For years, psychiatrists attributed obsessive-compulsive behaviors as a ritualized reaction to pervasive anxiety. Fromm discusses how a relationship can be distorted by anxiety:

> The frightened individual seeks somebody or something to tie his self to; he cannot bear to be his own individual self any longer, and tries frantically to get rid of it, and to feel security again by the elimination of this burden. (Fromm, 1960)

This explains the behavior of "woke" obsessionals during the pandemic. To alleviate their anxious concerns, they have been willing to divest themselves of their freedom in return for false protections offered by the government, masks, vaccines, etc.

For similar reasons, Progressive physicians also tend to adopt masochistic positions. It will undoubtedly sound extreme to suggest that physicians can be a masochistic group, but it is not. Indeed, masochistic impulses could explain why physicians are eager to identify with the "oppressed." Physicians are expected to care for the sick, and they derive little joy from the task. They accept this burden as a higher moral calling, which qualifies them as *moral masochists*, willing to sacrifice themselves for the needs of others.[64] Physicians have learned to put their wishes aside and to respond to the demands of others—parents, teachers, family, and patients. So, it is not surprising that they identify with the "oppressed" in society.

In *Escape from Freedom*, Fromm considered masochism a core feature of the "authoritarian personality." As he wrote:

> The different forms which masochistic strivings assume have one aim: to get rid of the individual self, to lose oneself; in other words, to get rid of the burdens of freedom ...Can we assume that by mak-

---

64 There are many examples of moral masochism in myth and literature. One that comes to mind is Sydney Carton in Dickens' *Tale of Two Cities*, in which Carton, a drunkard substitutes himself on the guillotine for his lookalike, the nobleman Charles Darnay.

ing a fear worse one is trying to remedy it? Indeed, that is what the masochistic person does.... If I succeed in reducing my individual self to nothing, if I can overcome my awareness of my separateness as an individual, I may save myself from this conflict. (Fromm, 1960)

This also may help to explain the recent willingness of Progressive physicians to favor the well-being of the group at the expense of individual rights.

In *On Liberty*, John Stuart Mill, a major source of the philosophy of Liberalism, elucidates his ideas concerning individual rights (Mill, 2002). Mill introduces the principle of "harm" and suggests that the rights of the individual should be limited only when they harm others. Mill makes a critical distinction between "harm" and "offense." For Mill, harm impedes on the rights or person of another. Examples of harm can range from putting the health of one's neighbor at risk to not paying taxes because the government relies on the money to take care of its citizens. On the other hand, an offense is something that might "hurt our feelings" but no more. According to Mill, offense is a less serious infraction, and no efforts should be made to prevent it. In this regard, Mill would deplore "politically correct" speech, as he viewed free speech as necessary for both intellectual and social progress. If free speech were to be prevented, according to Mill, progress would not occur, and therefore harm would be done. Progressives have adopted Mill's concept of "harm," but they have equated "offense" with it. This allows them to justify limiting speech that they find offensive.

Progressive physicians have focused on interventions that protect the public health at the expense of individual liberty based on the notion of "harm." They justify mandating vaccines by claiming that the unvaccinated harm others. Whereas in the past, it was a patient's choice as to whether he chose to receive a vaccination, today Progressive physicians argue that it is more important to protect the "vulnerable" in society.

But their thinking is flawed. It fails to take into account that the vaccines have been ineffective with respect to protecting others from contracting COVID-19 and that mask mandates have not protected others from "harm" either. Theoretical "harm" does not equate to real "harm" and, according to Mill, in the absence of evidence of real harm, there is no basis for limiting the liberty of others. The willingness to equate the abstract with the real is a feature that runs through Progressive thought and makes it ultimately untenable. Instead, those who choose to be vaccinated and to wear masks have every right to do so, but those who choose not to are in the right as well. Physicians who supported these mandates and the penalties imposed on those who refused to comply with them have sacrificed their credibility, and will not be trusted in the future.

THINKING WITHOUT BORDERS

Jung warned that the plasticity of the human psyche is limited. The human psyche has a long evolutionary history, and it includes irrational impulses that differ little from those of our ancient forebears. Rational cognition is only one capacity of the human mind, and when it is overdeveloped, it can lead to abstractions that diverge from what is possible. A mathematician may engage with numbers in ways that have no parallel in nature, but no harm will come from his activities.

The left brain that mediates analytical cognition is joined to an ontogenetically older right brain that is the source of the imaginal capacities of the psyche. Imagination precedes and underpins progress. But while certain imaginings presage progress, others lead nowhere. This is what distinguishes visionary science fiction from dead-end ideas. As a species, we have grown reliant on cognitive function. But excessive thinking is also a characteristic of obsessional neurosis (R. Kradin, 2012). Excessive thinking tends to restrict effects, making it inaccessible and thereby reducing feelings to a vestigial mental capacity. But feelings are important, especially for decision making. As the neuroscientist Antonio Damasio has demonstrated, in their absence, the ability to make sound decisions may be impossible. (Damasio, 2021)

Enamored with ideas and weak on feeling, Progressives are willing to accept, without evidence, the cognitive fantasy that man has the capacity to live peacefully with others without constraints. This argument has been going on for centuries and was framed by the conflict between Thomas Hobbes' *Leviathan* and Jean-Jacques Rousseau's *Social Contract.* As the social critic Thomas Sowell notes, Progressive vision is unconstrained, rooted in nonsequiturs and abstract utopian fantasies, such as Rousseau's "noble savage." (Sowell, 2007)

The Progressive visionary, Yuval Noah Hariri, suggests in *Sapiens* that what makes man unique is his ability to construct "imagined realities" (Hariri, 2015). Hariri is right but only to a point. When imagined realities are not firmly rooted in natural law, they may become destructive, like Mary Shelley's *Frankenstein*'s monster. We have entered a new age—one characterized by impressive discoveries. The Internet, artificial intelligence, and molecular biology are changing how we live. In *Homo Deus*, Hariri argues that man may now be poised to surpass the limits of nature and that if immortality is one day achieved, certain elites may well be the first to experience *apotheosis* (Hariri, 2020). Such ideas are applauded by Progressives like Bill Gates and Barack Obama. In recent years, elites have accumulated great wealth as a result of these new technologies, and they imagine even greater possibilities for the future. But some would term this is what the ancient Greeks termed *hubris*, what today might be termed "malignant narcissism," and are rightfully wary concerning what these elites have in mind for tour future. Those research scientists, including Dr. Fauci, who imagined that "gain of function" research on coronaviruses might be beneficial have much to answer for, and we are right not to trust them.

How should progress be assessed? Which of the competing cultural narratives should we choose to adopt in its pursuit? I suggest that change qualifies as progress only when it meets two criteria. First, does it comport with human nature? Second, does it ultimately promote well-being? When Progressives imagine a utopia, are they conjuring a world that we would want to live in? Progressive notions of utopia have never been demonstrated to be compatible with human nature, and efforts at creating them have left people demotivated and unhappy. This would not meet the proposed criteria for genuine progress. Indeed, it is likely the case that only narratives consonant with human nature has the potential to result in well-being. Religious traditions suggest and science confirms that people grow unhappy when they are dissatisfied, and dissatisfaction results from the discordance between expectation and reality (Sapolsky, 2017). If well-being is a reasonable goal for assessing progress, then the cultural narratives we adopt should enhance it.

It is impossible to know what drives man to strive to make progress. Darwinian evolution may be derivative of some unknown greater force in nature that seeks change. Something impels us to imagine new possibilities, many of which lead to dead ends, while others will successfully open new doors. Nature may be willing to tolerate many errors in its unknown desire to identify new paths forward.

At the same time, it is arguably man's role to "cultivate and care" for what we have been given. This attitude is the essence of Conservative philosophy, which seeks to retain what is good while continuously adapting it to new circumstances. It differs from the current Progressive stance rooted in Marxist deconstruction that offers no viable path forward because they refuse to accept human nature.

Unfortunately, drawing attention to these failures will not diminish Progressive optimism. It is a fixed idea, an intractable illusion. Few will willingly accept that their perspective on reality is faulty, for to admit as much is to experience the shame of being seriously flawed. The notion that Progressivism *is* a mental illness is not far-fetched, if adherence to the "reality principle" is judged to be a criterion for mental health.

HYPOCRISY

As previously noted, I had several colleagues who held conservative views when it was still acceptable to do so but who now espouse the Progressive "party line." Their change in attitude occurred virtually overnight, when they were apparently "born again." I note this, not simply to suggest that their newfound "wokeness" is hypocritical—although it is— but with the strong suspicion that they have no convictions. For most of their lives, they have succeeded by acting like chameleons, like the protagonist of Woody Allen's *Zelig*. What they are exceptionally good at is assessing the expectations of others and calculating which behaviors will serve them best. In this regard, they are consummate survivors, as to adopt conservative positions in the corporate hospital today is a dangerous dead end.

I was asked in a radio interview whether I thought that the Progressive ideological trends in medicine might be reversed in the future. My answer was that if there were to be a sudden sea change in the culture, most physicians would quickly be on board with it and that their current adherence to Progressive ideas would melt away. This should come as little surprise to those versed in the dark side of the history of the medical profession. Physicians have played a checkered role in past political movements. As part of the elite class, many chose

227

to identify with the ruling elite. In the *Nazi Doctors*, Robert Lifton discussed the nefarious role that physicians played in the atrocities of the Third Reich (Lifton, 2000). During that time, physicians engaged in shocking human experimentation including the design of death camps.

But a physician who allows ideology to influence his medical practice is no longer functioning as a physician. Personal ideological views *must* be kept apart from medical practice. As the current response to the coronavirus pandemic demonstrates, science and "wokeness" do not mix. I am of the opinion that many physicians, if given their druthers, would be happy not to participate in what is taking place either culturally or politically at the workplace, and would prefer to maintain a safe focus on their medical practice and research. But the current mode of authoritarian Progressivism is bullying physicians into conforming. Attuned to expectations, physicians feel "pressured" to be on what they have been cautioned is the virtuous side of the culture war. In addition, most have learned through a long process of indoctrination that there are generally no rewards in bucking the system. Unfortunately, courage and conviction are not their forte.

CONCLUSION

Without justice, courage is weak.

—Benjamin Franklin in *Poor Richard's Almanac*

The transformation of the medical profession over the last thirty years has in some respects been slow, but in the last four years, it has rapidly become more political, more "woke," more authoritarian, and less credible. Virtually everyone has been touched by the greed of the corporate health system and the tentacles of Progressivism that have infiltrated our politics and educational processes, now for over a century (R. Kradin, 2020). Traditional post-Enlightenment Liberalism has been transformed by a Progressive movement tainted by its nexus with Marxism. The Democratic Party, the primary political vehicle for the Progressive agenda, has shifted its emphasis from liberal concerns and the state of the working man to one aligned with corporate globalism and authoritarianism, and it may be on the verge of getting much worse should the "Great Reset" be achieved in the future.

Post-Enlightenment Liberalism traditionally shared critical elements with Progressivism. Both viewed science as a medium for societal improvement, and both shared an optimistic world-view that imagined man as potentially perfectible. But today, Progressivism imagines a utopian world in which nation, family, and religion, must be expunged before aspirations for universal brotherhood are realized.

Superficially, Progressivism has appeal, and it is easy to see why young, naïve, and idealistic physicians might want to promote it. Medicine has for years been invested in scientific progress, without concerns for race, gender, or nationality. An example of a Progressive medical organization is *Médecins Sans Frontieres* (MSF) (Doctors Without Borders), a humanitarian effort founded in the 1970s in response to the famine in Biafra. MSF originally focused on medical deprivation in "third world countries," but over time has championed transcending national borders.

At first, anti-Communist in its leanings, MSF has increasingly adopted the agenda of neoliberalism and globalism:

> The rejection of ideology as a justification of violence, if not its very source, as well as the desire to involve the media are two points in common between "New Philosophy" and "sans-frontiérisme." Thus, the originality of sans-frontiérisme within the humanitarian sector then laid in the increasing emphasis on calling into question state sovereignty and in its use of advocacy on behalf of victims. (F. Thomas, 2020)

But the "no borders" movement neglects the problems that would ensue in a borderless world. Be it "open borders," "defund the police movements," "transgenderism," the denial of "race," or genetic determinism, Progressive ideology insists on denying nature.

But it is unlikely that nature will accept the imposition of such fantasies for very long. Nature tends to reject what does not conform to *its* will. The fall of the Soviet Union was not primarily due to economics or to America's strength, rather it was the re-emergence of man's need to be free of tyranny and of the dehumanizing notion of "equity."

While a global economy may suit large corporations and their shareholders, it does not sit well with workers who must live within the borders of a nation. Progressivism's efforts at "deconstructing" the nuclear family have been attempted in the past, e.g., in Soviet Russia and in Israel, without success. And despite a crazed focus on diversity, there are limits to what most people will accept with respect to the re-imaginings of gender for their families.

Despite what may appear to be the case today, physicians who choose to align with Progressive ideology are on the *wrong* side both of the culture wars and history. Physicians are entrusted to serve as empirical observers of nature. When a conflict occurs between ideology and nature, the rightful place of the physician is on nature's side, and they discredit themselves when they make any other choice.

When physicians accept the irrational notion that it is acceptable for migrants—an unknown number of whom are infected with COVID-19 and other communicable diseases—to cross the border illegally and potentially infect other , or choose to excuse large gatherings during a pandemic because they are protesting perceived social injustices, they deny their medical and ethical responsibilities.

For many years, I worked in a large city emergency room where I saw the ravages of crime and addiction first hand. During that time, I worked closely with the police, who were often the first line of response for these issues, and developed an abiding respect for their courage and dedication. Physicians today who agree with the notion that the police should be defunded have not sufficiently pondered the ill effects that such policies are having on the health of the communities they serve.

Physicians who support gender reassignment surgeries for minor children have not adequately considered its physical and mental complications, and are morally, if not legally, responsible for them.

With respect to the current pandemic, physicians who continue to support the advice coming from our health policy leaders have done a disservice to the patients they were meant to serve. When the current pandemic first began, it was understandably difficult to know what advice was best. But that time is past, and each day reveals how wrong and deceptive our health leaders, media, and government have been on the topic. Physicians who support this charade have contributed to illness, despair, and societal chaos.

It should be obvious to any thoughtful physician that Dr. Fauci has little credibility with respect to how to handle the present pandemic. According to Fauci, due to the emergence of the omicron variant, it is still not safe to fly on an airplane without a mask, his rationale being that masks add an additional level of defense. But Fauci has not offered a shred of evidence to support that opinion. While science requires evidence, he apparently does not—except when it is convenient, as in the HCQ debacle.

In testimony to Congress, two airline executives from Delta and Southwest Airlines testified that wearing masks on airplanes is unnecessary:

> Kirby spoke of partnering with the Cleveland Clinic and how the Department of Defense tested airflow on United's airplanes. "And the conclusion of that is that effectively anywhere that you're going to be indoors, the airplane is the safest place that you can be indoors, it's because of the air filtration," said the United CEO. Next, Wicker deftly linked air filtration with the face mask mandate. "Will we ever, do you think, be able to get on an airplane without masks?" the senator asked of Southwest Airlines CEO Gary Kelly and American Airlines CEO Doug Parker. Kelly echoed the other CEOs' comments on air quality, noting that his airline partners with UT Southwestern and Stanford School of Medicine. "Yeah, I think the case is very strong that masks don't add much if anything in the air cabin environment. It is very safe, and very high quality compared to any other indoor setting." "I concur," said Parker. "The aircraft is the safest place you can be. It's true of all of our aircraft, they all have these HEPA filters and the same airflow." (Kelleher, 2021)

I do not make a habit of taking medical advice from corporate executives, but they have little reason to fabricate or exaggerate their position on wearing masks. If anything, they risked criticism from other globalist CEOs who support the Biden administration's mask mandates. But these two airline CEOs were reportedly on the verge of retirement and intent on speaking the truth as they understood it. Furthermore, they provided a sound scientific basis for their opinion, which is more than Fauci did. The evidence shows that masks do nothing to stop the transmission of viruses beyond the air filtration systems of the airplane.

When as a physician, I must choose the advice of airline executives over the head of America's Coronavirus Task Force, it's a sad day for medicine. But where are the other physicians who must also know better? How many "breakthrough cases" amongst the vaccinated must be documented before they admit that the current vaccine strategies are not protective? When will they acknowledge that masks are ineffective and have potentially done harm to young children who are forced to wear them needlessly? Why have they not insisted on seeing the data that supports the conclusion that the vaccinated are protected against severe disease, as opposed to the more likely possibility that the current mutant strains are simply less virulent?

What was the need for mass viral testing? What was the rationale for administering "boosters" with vaccines that neither protect against infection nor the transmission of virus? Certainly, any knowledgeable physician with clinical experience and common sense must realize that the counsel coming from Fauci is baseless. When will physicians insist that the origins of SARS-CoV2 be seriously investigated over Fauci's objections? In other words, what will it take for America's physicians to acknowledge that the "emperor has no clothes?"

As this text has examined, the failures of the medical profession have been in the making for some time, but during the present pandemic, they have been legion. Medicine has become yet another victim of a culture that has lost its way. The ethical basis and practice of medicine have been corroded by ideology, greed, and corruption. Few physicians today contemplate the ethical demands of their profession. Instead, a shallow allegiance to "social justice" has replaced a thoughtful comprehension of a physician's role in society.

In times of medical crisis, such as the present pandemic, physicians are expected to rise to the occasion, not only with respect to the delivery of health care but also as sources of credible information for the public. They are morally obligated to assess risk objectively, to inspire confidence when the evidence indicates that it is appropriate, and not to raise anxieties needlessly.

Physicians are expected to question data and not to disseminate propaganda, no matter what the "official" source. And when they consider data, they should also take into account the reliability of its source. Despite their penchant for deferring to authority, they must conjure up the mettle to question the counsel of health officials when appropriate, and put selfish concerns for career aside, when they interfere with their ethical obligation to patients.

Is there a remedy for the current situation that the medical profession finds itself in? The answer is yes, but it will require major changes in the system. Change needs to begin with the education of the young. Any ideology that preaches what to believe should not be a piece of education at any level. Children should be exposed to facts, taught *how* to think, never *what* to think.

Criteria for acceptance into medical schools should be reconsidered. Today, medical school admissions are almost exclusively based on academic performance and scores on standardized tests. But one does not have to be a stellar student to be an excellent physician. Most physicians will not become stellar medical researchers, and even this group will not be accurately identified based solely on previous academic performance. The creativity that distinguishes a great researcher from a mediocre one cannot be ascertained based on test scores. The medical school committees that screen applicants should consider criteria other than grades, and more importantly, spend time interviewing applicants in an effort to discern their character. Of course, if the members of the admission committee are themselves mediocre, it is unlikely that they will make good choices.

The current single-minded emphasis on math and science in pre-medical education tends to exclude applicants who would likely make excellent physicians. Pre-medical courses should include history, language, social sciences, etc., which will enhance the knowledge of a well-rounded physician. Character traits including empathy, honesty, and moral courage, are essential qualities in a physician, and they should not be ignored, lest we turn out generations of science nerds who are unable to relate to the psychological needs of patients.

Nevertheless, admission to medical school, and subsequently to residency training programs, should be based primarily on merit. While there is a place for diversity in training due to the needs of different medical communities, "identity" is never a substitute for merit. Thomas Sowell has noted that failure to match the quality of the student to the quality of the educational institution is a cause of unnecessary academic failure:

> Minority students who did not meet the academic standards at Berkeley and UCLA were not "unqualified." Most were well qualified to be in college, but somewhere else. The University of California-Irvine was one of those other institutions where they could be admitted legitimately, without any double standards.

The average white high school graduate would not succeed at Berkeley or UCLA—but only the top tier of white students are admitted. It is only minority students who are likely to be admitted to institutions where they are likely to fail....

Instead of failing at Berkeley or UCLA, these students have a much better chance of succeeding at UC-Irvine or Cal State-Hayward. Instead of having to take sop courses in order to survive at institutions where the pace is too much for them, they can take solid courses elsewhere that will prepare them for a worthwhile occupation or give them a solid foundation for postgraduate work.

It should take just one graduating class admitted without academic double standards to expose the fraud of affirmative action. When minority students begin graduating at a higher rate than before and are able to hold their own academically with their white classmates, it should become clear to any fair-minded person that racial quotas were a bad mistake and that equal opportunity makes everybody better off.

But those who have been pushing affirmative action all these years do not want their dogmas put to the test and discredited....

In other words, any group that does not score as high as other groups is being discriminated against. Does this make any sense? Different groups have had different test scores all around the world. With or without test scores, they have also had different academic performances. (Sowell, 1999)

The current emphasis on "social justice" in medical education is misguided and must end. As previously noted, whatever discrepancies do exist in the delivery of health care to "people of color" are not solely attributed to "systemic racism," as there are multiple contributory reasons for discrepancies. Poor people of *any* color are more likely to receive suboptimal care, due to obstacles on both sides of the doctor-patient equation. When it is simplistically assumed that "racism" is the cause of inferior health outcomes, other factors that should be attended to will remain unaddressed. Such research should be conducted by disinterested investigators, not "social justice warriors." For their own future benefit, minorities and the poor must ultimately be held responsible and accountable for their actions. Supporting a culture of victimization serves no one's interests. It purposely obscures underlying racism, and truth should never be sacrificed on the altar of ideology.

Virtue signaling has *no* place in the practice of medicine. Sincere concern for others is an essential part of being a physician. Singling out *any* group for special attention ignores the physician's duty to remain blind to race, wealth, and status when providing care. And real virtue is lived, not signaled.

The lifelong practice of medicine is a study in the merits and foibles of man. It requires empathy and sensitivity to the human condition. Progressive "wokeness" is not, as some would like to believe, evidence of increased awareness and sensitivity. Rather, it is a superficial and often insincere response to a *zeitgeist* that physicians should not engage in.

All medicine is "local." Physicians do not treat groups or "identities." Rather, their focus should be on the needs of the patient in front of them. Global concerns are too distant and divorced from everyday realities to be genuinely felt. Whereas "global warming" may currently be influencing health in some parts of the globe, those qualified to address the health effects of climate change represent a small and specialized group. The average physician is in no position to evaluate what is true or false concerning global warming or its health effects. Instead, a physician's most effective and proper role is to address patients within their purview, not to engage as an activist in climatological controversy.

The current health establishment is corrupt and should be purged, as soon as possible, of all influences of ideology, politics, and financial gain. Once venerable societies like the AMA have lost sight of their purpose, which is to optimize American health-care delivery. When these agencies choose sides in the culture wars and preach propaganda, they have forfeited their authority. Many of the recent positions taken by major medical societies have been unethical. Physicians are supposed to advise their patients, not demand behavioral changes for ideological or any other purposes. Most patients are mentally sound consenting adults, and in a free country, they should never be forced to receive *any* medical treatment against their wishes, unless they present a *clear and present danger* to the health of others. Should that possibility arise, the standards for determining what represents an acute threat must remain high. For a disease like COVID-19 that results in severe illness and death in well less than 1 percent of the population, it is impossible to argue that a standard has been met to mandate precautionary treatments.

Definitions matter and should not be subject to political whims. This was discussed in an opinion piece concerning a recent influenza pandemic, but it applies to the current coronavirus crisis as well:

> A pandemic is defined as "an epidemic occurring worldwide, or over a very wide area, crossing international boundaries and usually affecting a large number of people." The classical definition includes nothing about population immunity, virology or disease severity....

> It is tempting to surmise that the complicated pandemic definitions used by the World Health Organization (WHO) and the Centers for Disease Control and Prevention of the United States of America involved severity in a deliberate attempt to garner political attention and financial support for pandemic preparedness ...conflating spread and severity allowed the suggestion that 2009 A (H1N1) was not a pandemic. It was, in fact, a classical pandemic, only much less severe than many had anticipated or were prepared to acknowledge, even as the evidence accumulated. (Kelly, 2011)

Dr. Fauci has garnered substantial funding for the NIAID by exaggerating the scope and severity of a variety of infectious diseases during his tenure at NIH, and there is reason to believe that he has taken advantage of the present pandemic for a similar purpose (Kennedy Jr., 2021). But pandemics do not last forever; they have a limited lifetime, and public health experts must recognize and inform the public when a pandemic has "burned itself out." In the case of viral pandemics, most do so by becoming *endemic* infections. As Dr. Michael Ryan, the Executive Director of the WHO Health Emergency Program, suggests:

> I think it's important to put this on the table: this virus (COVID-19) may just become another endemic virus in our communities. And this virus may never go away. HIV has not gone away, but we've come to terms with the virus, and we have found the therapies and we have found the prevention methods, and people don't feel as scared as they did before. And we're offering life—long, healthy life—to people with HIV. And I'm not comparing the two diseases, but I think it is important that we be realistic. And I don't think anyone can predict when or if this disease will disappear. (Gartz, 2021)

A pandemic in practice will tend to last only as long as the fear that it generates. There is optimism that the current pandemic is in the process of transmuting into an endemic infection, based on diminished death rates, the large vaccinated population, and available therapies. But there is no reason to believe that the COVID-19 virus will be eradicated. Rather, it will more likely continue to re-visit us as a seasonal infection that leads to mild illness and with limited mortality in highly vulnerable populations.

Dr. Walensky was recently criticized for suggesting that it is those with "four or more" serious risk factors who are at risk of dying from COVID-19 because her position was judged as "callous." But it is time for anxious "woke" critics to come to grips with death. Old people die; sick people die; and unless human biology changes radically in the future, *everyone* will die And yes, people *die*; they don't *pass on*. Physicians of all people should not shy away from talking frankly about death. It is neither callous nor "harsh" to acknowledge this; instead, to object to the use of the term *death* is prima facie evidence of neurosis.

For the present pandemic to end, our public health and government leaders will need to recognize, admit, and inform the public that the acute danger is over. Based on the handling of the pandemic until now, it is likely that our public health officials will remain slow to do this, for reasons unrelated to public health. In *Doom*, the historian, Niall Ferguson, discusses conditions that have led to catastrophes in the past. He explains how the 1957 pandemic of Asian Flu was addressed by the Eisenhower administration and compares that to how the current COVID-19 pandemic has been handled. The Asian influenzavirus affected the entire world; it killed ~1.1 million,[65] and was particularly lethal for young adults in the prime of their lives. Unlike the public health response to COVID-19:

> Eisenhower did not declare a state of emergency in 1957. There were no state lockdowns and no school closures. Sick students simply stayed at home, as they usually did. Work continued more or less uninterrupted. Nor did the Eisenhower administration borrow to the hilt to fund transfers and loans to citizens and businesses. The President asked Congress for a mere $2.5 million ($23 million in today's inflation-adjusted terms, and around 0.0005 percent of the 1957 GDP which was $474 billion) to provide additional help to the Public Health Service. (N. Ferguson, 2021)

A medical team at Bethesda Hospital rapidly developed a vaccine and began administering it. The economic consequences of the pandemic were, as Ferguson termed them, "miniscule."

The implications of this comparison are clear. They amount to an indictment of the health policies adopted by medical professionals and politicians for the present pandemic. But the public is by no means free of its share of blame. The current culture lacks courage, competence,

---

65 At current world population density, it is estimated that the Asian flu would result in 2.7 million deaths if it visited us today.

and common sense. It is a society in decline—one led to the brink of ruin by narcissism, arrogance, greed, and fear.

Perhaps it is too much to expect America's leaders to rise above the toxic influences of the present culture. After all, 1957 was a very different time, and it is not possible to bring back the past. But if we are to survive, the current trajectory of the culture and specifically of the medical profession *must* change.

In the nineteenth century, journalist Emile Zola confronted injustice in French society during the anti-Semitic Dreyfuss affair. In that spirit, *I accuse* Dr. Fauci and his colleagues at the NIH, the head of the CDC, the mainstream media, *Big Tech*, *Big Pharma*, globalist corporations, the Biden administration, the Democratic Party, and the Teachers Union, of perversely manipulating the coronavirus pandemic for their own benefits. *I accuse* those academic physicians, major medical journals, and medical societies, who abandoned their mission to the public and to science, and who provided only silence in the face of obvious misinformation and lies. They deserve to be singled out because they, more than anyone else, were qualified to recognize what was transpiring and to speak out against it. Their refusal to do so has damaged the credibility of the medical profession, and it is questionable whether public trust in it can be restored.

BIBLIOGRAPHY

AACC. (2020). SARS CoV2 cycle threshold: a metric that matters or not.

Adam, D. (2020). Hydroxychloroquine. *Nature*.

Aeyung, B., Baron-Cohen, S., E., S., & et al. (2009). Fetal testosterone predicts sexually differentiated childhood in boys and girls. *Psychological Science, 20*, 144-148.

AHRQ. (2021). What Is Patient Experience?

AMA. (2020). Joint statement on ordering, prescribing or dispensing COVID-19 medications.

AMA. (2021). AMA to states: Stop interfering in health care of transgender children.

Andrzejewski, A. (2019). Top U.S. "Non-Profit" Hospitals & CEOs Are Racking Up Huge Profits. *Forbes*.

Angell, M. (2009). *Conflicts of interest that undermine the goals of academic medicine and harm the public.*, Harvard Medical School.

Archer, S. (2020). 5 failings of the Great Barrington Declaration's dangerous plan for COVID-19 natural herd immunity. *The Conversation*.

Atlas, S. (2021). *A Plague on Both Their Houses*. New York: Bombadier.

Atlas, S. (2021). *A Plague Upon Our House*. Nashville: Post Hill Press.

Bader, C., Baker, J, Day, E., & Gordon, A. (2021). The Causes and Consequences of Fear in America. *Chapman University*.

Becker, E. (1973). *Denial of Death*. New York: Free Press.

Beigel, J., Tomashek, K., Dodd, L., & et al. (2020). Remdesivir for the Treatment of Covid-19 - Final Report. *NEJM, 383*, 1813-1828.

Berenson, A. (2020). *Unreported Truths About Covid-19 and Lockdowns*. New York: Blue Deep, Inc.

Berenson, A. (2021). *Pandemia*. New York: Regnery.

Boyd, J. (2021). Kids are more at risk of dying from seasonal flu but the CDC says that they should get the jab anyway. *Conservative Review*.

Bryant, A., Lawrie, T., & Dowswell, T. (2021).

Ivermectin for Prevention and Treatment of COVID-19 Infection: A Systematic Review, Meta-analysis, and Trial Sequential Analysis to Inform Clinical Guidelines. *American Journal of Therapeutics:, 28*.

Caffrey, M. (2021). Study Reveals Declining Life Expectancy Among White Americans That Defies Easy Answers. *AJMC*.

Caldwell, C. (2020). *Age of Entitlement*. New York: Simon & Schuster.

Canales, K. (2021). China's 'social credit' system ranks citizens and punishes them with throttled internet speeds and flight bans if the Communist Party deems them untrustworthy. *Insider*.

Carroll, C. (2021). The American Medical Association goes woke. *Washington Examiner*.

Center for Gender Surgery Boston Children's Hospital. (2021).

Chakraborty, B. (2020). China hints at denying Americans life-saving coronavirus drugs.

Cohen, C., & Kupferschmidt, K. (2020). The 'very, very bad look' of remdesivir, the first FDA-approved COVID-19 drug. *Science*.

Cristofari, S., Bertrand, B., Leuzzi, S., & al, e. (2019). Postoperative complications of male to female sex reassignment surgery: a 10-year French retropsective study. *Ann Chir Past Esthet, 64*, 24-32.

Dai, L., & Gao, G. (2020). Viral targets for vaccines against COVID-19. *Nature Reviews Immunology, 21*, 73-82.

Damasio, A. (2021). *Feeling and Knowing*. New York: Pantheon.

Di'Souza, D. (2020). *United States of Socialism*. New York: All Points Books.

Dickson, E. (2021). How Joe Rogan Became a Cheerleader for Ivermectin.

Ebina-Shibuya, R., Namkoong, H., Horita, N., & al, e. (2021). Hydroxychloroquine and chloroquine for treatment of coronavirus disease 19 (COVID-19): a systematic review and meta-analysis of randomized and non-randomized controlled trials. *J Thorac Dis., 13*, 202-212.

Editor. (2021). NIH says grantee failed to report experiment in Wuhan that .made mice sicker. *Science*.

Farris, A. (2021). Yale Epidemiologist Says COVID-19 Fear 'Manufactured" by Authorities. *Outkick*.

Ferguson, C. (2021). *How Madness Shaped History*. New York: Prometheus Books.

Ferguson, N. (2011). *Civilization*. New York: Penguin.

Ferguson, N. (2021). *Doom*. New York: Penguin.

Fraire, A., 'Woda, B., Kradin, R. L., & al, e. (2016). *Viruses and the Lung: Infections and Non-Infectious Viral-Linked Lung Disorders*. New York: Springer.

Frankfurt, H. (2006). *On Bullshit*. Princteon: Princeton University Press.

Freud, S. (1907). Obsessive Actions and Religious Practices. In J. Strachey (Ed.), *Standard Edition of the Collected Works of Sigmund Freud* (Vol. IX). London: Hogarth.

Fromm, E. (1960). *Escape from Freedom.* New York: Vintage.

Galiatsatos, P. (2021). COVID-19 Lung Damage. *Johns Hopkins Medicine.*

Garber, J. (2019). Why you should be a "medical conservative".

Gartz, M. (2021). What Does It Mean for a Virus to Become 'Endemic?'.

Gautret, P., J, L., P., P., & al, e. (2020). Hydroxychloroquine and azithromycin as a treatment of COVID-19: results of an open-label non-randomized clinical trial. *Int J Antimicrob Agents., 56.*

Genieys, W., & Brown, L. (2020). Fact check U.S.: Can Joe Biden really 'stop the virus' in the U.S. as he claims? *The Conversation.*

Griffin, R. (2021). Pfizer Boosts Forecast for Vaccine Sales to $33.5 Billion. *Bloomberg News.*

Haidt, J. (2013). *The Rigtheous Mind.* New York: Vintage.

Hariri, Y. N. (2015). *Sapiens.* New York: Harper.

Hariri, Y. N. (2018). *21 Lessons for the 21st Century.* New York: Harper.

Hariri, Y. N. (2020). *Homo Deus.* New York: Harper.

Hemingway, M. (2021). *Rigged.* New York: Regenry.

Hensley, S. (2021). An FDA panel supports Merck COVID drug in mixed vote.

Hinton, D. (2020). *e Emergency Use Authorization (EUA) for emergency use of oral formulations*

of chloroquine phosphate (CQ) and hydroxychloroquine sulfate (HCQ) FDA

Horton, R. (2015). Offline: What is medicine's 5 sigma? *Lancet, 285,* 315.

Hospitals get paid more to list patients as COVID-19. (2020).

Hydroxychloroquine. (2021).

Jefferson, T., & Jones, M. (2020). Physical interactions to interrupt or reduce the spread of respiratory vfiruses. *MedRXiv* Joseph, S. (2013). Patients or Clients?

Jung, C. G. (1949). *On the Psychology of the Unconscious* (Vol. 7). Princeton: Princeton.

Jung, C. G. (1962). *Archetypes and the Collective Unconscious* (Vol. 9i). Princeton: Princeton.

Kelleher, R. (2021). Airline CEOs Tell Congress We Don't Need Masks On Planes, Get Factchecked By Flight Attendant Union President. *Forbes.*

Kelly, H. (2011). The classical definition of a pandemic is not elusive. *Bull World Health Organ., 89,* 540-541.

Kennedy Jr., R. F. (2021). *The Real Anthony Fauci*. New York: Skyhorse.

Keyes, R. (2016). *The Post-Truth Era: Dishonesty and Deception in Contemporary Life*. New York: St. Martins Press.

Koczkodaj, W., Masiak, J., Mazurek, M., & et al. (2019). *Massive Health Record Breaches Evidenced by the Office for Civil Rights Data* (Vol. 48).

Kohut, H. (1971). *he Analysis of the Self: A Systematic Approach to the Psychoanalytic Treatment of Narcissistic Personality Disorders*. New York: International Universities Press.

Kradin, R. (2008). *The Placebo Response*. New York: Routledge.

Kradin, R. (2012). *Pathologies of the Mind/Body Interface: Exploring the Curious Domain of the Psychosomatic Disorder*. New York: Routledge.

Kradin, R. (2017). *Surgical Pathology of Infectious Diseases*. New York: Elsevier.

Kradin, R. (2018). *Out of Control: Apocalyptic Psychology in the Age of Trump*. Boston: Amazon.

Kradin, R. (2020). *Breakdown: How Progressive Ideology is Undermining Morality and Redefining Mental Health in America*. Conroe: Defiance Press.

Kradin, R., Lazrus, D., Dubinett, S., & al, e. (1989). Tumour-infiltrating lymphocytes and interleukin-2 in treatment of advanced cancer. *Lancet, 333*, 577-580.

Kradin, R. L. (2004). The placebo response: its putative role as a functional salutogenic mechanism of the central nervous system. *Perspect Biol Med, 47*(3), 328-338. Retrieved from https://www.ncbi.nlm.nih.gov/pubmed/15247500

Krawczyk, F., & Kulczycki, E. (2021). How is open access accused of being predatory? The impact of Beall's lists of predatory journals on academic publishing. *he Journal of Academic Librarianship, 47*.

Kuhn, T. (1962). *Structure of Scientific Revolution*. Chicago: University of Chicago.

Lasch, C. (1979). *The Culture of Narcissism: American Life in an Age of Diminishing Expectations*. New York: W.W. Norton.

Li, D. (2021). Youth suicide attempts soared during pandemic, CDC report says.

Lifton, R. J. (2000). *The Nazi doctors : medical killing and the psychology of genocide : with a new preface by the author* (2000 ed.). New York: Basic Books.

Lukianoff, G., & Haidt, J. (2015). Coddling of the American Mind. *Atlantic*.

Mandavilli, A. (2022). The C.D.C. Isn't Publishing Large Portions of the Covid Data It Collects.

Maragakis, L., & Kelen, G. (2021). Breakthrough Infections: Coronavirus After Vaccination. *John Hopkins*.

Martin, D. (2014). Dr. Arnold Relman, 91, Journal Editor and Health System Critic, Dies. *NY Times*.

McIntyre, L. (2015). *Respecting Truth*. New York: Routledge.

McLaughlin, D. (2022). American Slavery in the Global Context. *National Review, LXXIV,* 20-26.

McNally, R. (2012). *What is Mental Illness?* Cambridge: Harvard University Press.

Mehra, M., et al. (2020). Hydroxychloroquine or chloroquine with or without a macrolide for treatment of COVID-19: a multinational registry analysis. *Lancet, 6736,* 31324-31326.

Melnick, T. (2019). Yale study: Doctors give electronic health record an 'F'.

Menger, R. (2019). Non-Profit Hospitals Are Making a Killing.

Meyers, L. (2020). The psychological challenges of gender reassignment surgery. *APA, 38,* 52.

Mill, J. S. (2002). *On Liberty*. New York: Dover Thrift.

Morrisey, D. (2012). The True Costs of Alienating Patients. *Physcian Weekly*.

Murphy, J. (2021). The Real College Admissions Scandal. *Slate*.

Murray, C. (2012). *Coming Apart*. New York: CrownForum.

Myre, G. (2020). U.S. Officials: Beware Of China And Others Trying To Steal COVID-19 Research.

Ndugga , N., Hilll, L., Artiga, S., & Haldar, H. (2021). Latest Data on COVID-19 Vaccinations by Race/Ethnicity.

Nelson, S. (2019). *The Gap Between Rich And Poor Americans' Health Is Widening.*

NIH. (2021). Extramural Research Overview for Fiscal Year 2020.

Northrop, K. (2021). American Hospitals Take the China Road: *The Wire*.

Nutt, A. (2017). Long shadow cast by psychiatrist on transgender issues finally recedes at Johns Hopkins. *Washinton Post*.

Opinion, E. (2021). How Fauci and Collins Shut Down Covid Debate. *Wall Street Journal*.

Orwell, G. (1949). *1984*. London: Cheapest Books.

Poll, G. (2019). *Satisfaction with Health Care in the U.S.* Retrieved from Gallup Poll:

Porter, R. (2006). *Cambridge History of Medicine*. Cambridge: Cambridge University Press.

Quay, S. (2021). *New Study By Dr. Steven Quay Concludes that SARS-CoV-2 Came from a Laboratory.*

Ramaswarmy, V. (2021). *Woke, Inc.* New York: Center City.

Rindsberg, A. (2021). *The Gray Lady Winked*. Tel Aviv: Midnight Oil.

Rusu, M., & Herman, R. (2018). The Implications of propaganda as a social influence strategy. *Scientific Bulletin, 23.*

Sanger-Katz, M. (2016). Your Surgeon Is Probably a Republican, Your Psychiatrist Probably a Democrat. *NY Times.*

Sapolsky, R. (2017). *Behave: The Biology of Humans at Our Best and Worst.* New York: Penguin.

Schiff, S. (2015). *Witches.* New York: Back Bay Books.

Schoenberg, S. (2021). Healey says Mass General Brigham expansion will net $385m annual profit AG raises new questions about impacts on health care costs. *CommonWealth.*

Scruton, R. (2017). *Conservatism.* New York: All Points Books.

Segel, K. (2017). Bureaucracy Is Keeping Health Care from Getting Better. *Harvard Business Review.*

Sidik, S. (2022). Heart-disease risk soars after COVID — even with a mild case.

Sowell, T. (1999). The other side of affirmative action. *Sun.*

Sowell, T. (2007). *A Conflict of Visions.* New York: Basic Books.

Sowell, T. (2011). *The Thomas Sowell Reader.* New York: Basic Books.

Statista. (2021). Share of Americans who identify as LGBT from 2012 to 2020, by generation.

Tai-Seale, M., McGuire, T., & Zhang, W. (2007). Time Allocation in Primary Care Office Visits. *Health Serv Res, 42,* 1871-1894.

Taliesen, J. (2021). 'Don't do it': Dr. Fauci warns against using ivermectin to treat or prevent COVID-19.

Thomas, F. (2020). The borders of idealism? From third-worldism to "sans-frontiérisme". *Humanitarian Alternatives.*

Thomas, L. (2021). The origin of SARS-CoV-2 furin cleavage site remains a mystery.

Wadman, M. (2021). Israelis who had an infection were more protected against the Delta coronavirus variant than those who had an already highly effective COVID-19 vaccine. *Science.*

Wang, S. (2006). Sports Complex: The Science Behind Fanatic Behavior.

Williams, J., Krah, J., & et al (2020). The physiological burden of prolonged PPE use on health care workers during long shifts. *US Centers of Disease Control and Prevention.*

Zhong, D., Xiao, S., Debes, A., & et al. (2021). Durability of Antibody Levels After Vaccination With mRNA SARS-CoV-2 Vaccine in Individuals With or Without Prior Infection. *JAMA, 326,* 2524-2526\

INDEX